# AN
# INTRODUCTION
# TO
# THE SEC

K. FRED SKOUSEN

*Chairman, Department of Accounting*
*Graduate School of Management*
*Brigham Young University*

Published by
**SOUTH-WESTERN PUBLISHING CO.**

A09

CINCINNATI   WEST CHICAGO, ILL.   DALLAS   PELHAM MANOR, N.Y.
PALO ALTO. CALIF.   BRIGHTON, ENGLAND

# *PREFACE*

In a free enterprise economy, such as is found in the United States, continued growth and stability require a healthy flow of capital from private and institutional investors to the managements of business enterprises. Capital markets and private financing are the media in the U.S. by which the exchanges occur.

The Securities and Exchange Commission was established in 1934 in an effort to foster honest and open securities markets. Congress, in establishing the SEC, gave broad powers to the new commission to regulate securities and to ensure proper financial reporting and disclosure by American businesses.

The importance of the SEC and its dealings with the business community in general and the accounting profession in particular is, in the view of the author, unquestionable. Accounting and financial periodicals frequently carry announcements of some new accounting rule or the liability of an accountant or business executive under the Securities Acts. Many accounting, legal, and consulting firms derive a major part of their revenues from activities directly or indirectly related to the SEC. For accountants, these activities range from the certification of financial statements used in registrations under the various Securities Acts to the giving of advice on the applicability of different provisions of the Acts.

The purpose of this book, in a narrow sense, is to acquaint the reader with the nature, origin, and working of the SEC, particularly as related to the accounting profession. In a broader sense, this book deals with the informational needs and requirements relative to the capital markets. Hopefully, the reader will be able to see the relationship between investment decisions (by both investors and managers), capital markets regulation by the SEC, and the role of the accountant and business executive relative to both.

The book is structured to accomplish these purposes. The first chapter gives an historical background to securities legislation in the U.S. and explains the structure and work of the SEC. Chapter 2 looks at the legal framework of the SEC, with a brief explanation of each major act administered by the Commission. Also included is a description of the accountant's primary duties under each act. Chapter 3 focuses attention on the registration process and the reporting requirements, primarily under the 1933 and 1934 Acts. A comparative analysis between reports presented to shareholders and those submitted to the SEC is given in Chapter 4. A unique approach is taken in that actual case histories are presented to highlight the comparisons. The final chapter looks at the extensive interaction between the SEC and the business community, including liability under the Securities Acts and the present critical issue of determining generally accepted accounting principles. An appendix, containing an annotated bibliography, gives further guidance into SEC research and provides valuable information for those wishing to augment the material presented in this book.

In view of the impact of the SEC on business and the accounting profession, it seems strange that so little attention is given to the subject in the typical business and accounting curriculum. There are a few lengthy, technical books used by professionals on the subjects covered in this text. The bibliography provides selected references. This introductory text attempts to summarize detail and to synthesize technicalities in a readable, useful manner for accounting and business students. The more detailed books are not entirely suited for classroom instruction. Hopefully, this book will fill a perceived need for an introduction to the SEC.

Although intended primarily as a supplement to intermediate accounting, auditing, and accounting theory classes, the book can easily be used to provide an overview to the SEC and its importance to business in general. This is especially needed in graduate accounting or MBA programs where such exposure has not previously been provided. The book should establish a basis for further study and research on the separate topics described herein.

This book is the result of the efforts of many people. Personal gratitude and the principle of full and fair disclosure require that I acknowledge these contributions collectively, if not individually. Special recognition and thanks is given to J. Kent Millington who assisted significantly in the research and preparation of the text. Appreciation is also expressed to C. Fred Harlow of the Deseret Pharmaceutical Company for his cooperation and assistance in providing the case materials contained herein; to Jay Christensen and Meyer Gottlieb of Price Waterhouse and Co. for their review of the entire manuscript; to Arlene Kirby for typing and proofing innumerable drafts of the manuscript; and to numerous students and colleagues for their encouragement and assistance while writing the book. Notwithstanding the involvement of others, the responsibility for any deficiencies in this book must be assumed solely by the author.

*K. Fred Skousen*

# AN INTRODUCTION TO THE SEC
## CONTENTS

## Chapter 4
## A Comparative Analysis     53

## Chapter 5
## Impact of the SEC on the Accounting Profession and the Business Community     85

*Chapter* *1*   # ORIGIN AND NATURE OF THE SEC

The Securities and Exchange Commission (SEC) was established in 1934 to help regulate the United States securities market. Since that time, the SEC has played a very important role in the business community. This chapter deals with the reasons for the establishment of the SEC, its organizational structure, and its current operation. First, a brief discussion of the corporate form of business, capital markets, and the need for disclosure of financial information is required.

## HISTORICAL BACKGROUND

In the early days of commerce, the economic system was basically a barter economy. Goods and services were traded directly for other goods and services. Businesses were conducted as proprietorships or perhaps as partnerships and joint ventures. Generally, the management and the owners were the same individuals. External reporting of operations by these closely held commercial entities was simply not needed. Internal information for efficient control was needed, however, and accounting systems were introduced to help provide that information.

### Establishment and Early Regulation of Capital Markets

As commercial enterprises multiplied both in size and number, more and more people were attracted to business opportunities, and the investment of capital resources expanded rapidly. The more aggressive businesses soon realized the lucrative advantage of encouraging capital investment by people willing to assume the risks of ownership while being neither willing nor able to assist in management. An advantage of the developing corporate form of business was that ownership and financial interest could be spread over a broad base by issuing securities. Ownership and management thus became separated, and there was a need for a marketplace where equity and debt securities could be exchanged for invested capital resources. This need led to the establishment of extensive capital markets, first in Europe and then in the United States.

The corporate form of business also increased the need for objective verification of data and created a need for disclosure in the form of more and better information to owners and potential investors. As capital markets increased in size and activity, an irresponsible attitude developed in some corporate officers who took advantage of lax conditions in the securities markets and profited by distortions and manipulations. Governments, sensing some responsibility to protect those who invested in corporations, made faltering attempts to create a working partnership between management and investors and to ensure an adequate supply of capital available for sound economic growth.

For example, King Edward I, attempting to gain some control over burgeoning capital markets, in 1285 authorized the Court of Aldermen to license brokers located in London. In the early 18th century, France and England experienced a mania of speculative investment centered around the development of trading companies doing business in the Western Hemisphere. At one point, scheme offers exceeded £300,000,000 sterling in the aggregate — more than the value of all the land in Great Britain.[1] Parliament, incensed over the abuses, retaliated with the harsh Bubble Act of 1720, holding issuers and brokers liable for damages and losses resulting from dishonest issues of securities.

## Regulation of Securities in the U.S.

The pattern of securities legislation in the United States followed the example of Great Britain: widespread abuses, made obvious by a financial crisis, followed by a series of retrospective investigations

[1]Louis Loss, *Securities Regulation* (Boston: Little, Brown, & Co., 1961), p. 4.

leading to the passage of restrictive laws imposed on securities markets.

A popular misconception is that securities regulation in the United States stems only from the crash of the stock market in 1929 and the ensuing years of financial stagnation. The financial difficulties of the 1930s only provided the last straw, the impetus, to pass securities legislation in the United States.

**Early Federal Attempts.** Federal securities legislation had been sought since the late 19th century. In 1885, discussion concerned federal licensing of companies involved in interstate commerce. The Federal Trade Commission Act and the Clayton Act resulted from efforts at federal control during the first years of this century. The Industrial Commission, established by Congress in 1898, reported in 1902 that public disclosure of material information of all publicly held corporations should be mandatory, including annual financial reports. During the next two decades, three major bills seeking greater disclosure were introduced into Congress but none were ever reported out of committee to either the House or the Senate. The time was not right; a serious financial plight was not in recent memory to spur such legislation.

**State Regulation.** While the federal government was searching for its role in securities legislation, state governments were making some attempts to bring order to chaotic securities markets. Kansas led the way in 1911 to combat the bleeding of the "Agrarian West" by the "Moneyed East."[2] By 1913, 22 other states had passed similar laws aimed at regulating the sale of securities. Divided into two categories, these laws were: (1) fraud laws, which imposed penalties if evidence indicated fraud had been committed in the sale of securities; and (2) regulatory laws, which attempted to prohibit the sale of securities until an application was filed and permission was granted by the state.[3] These early laws became known as "blue-sky" laws after a judicial decision characterized some transactions as "speculative schemes that have no more basis than so many feet of blue sky."[4]

State laws, for several reasons, never proved really effective in regulating the securities market. Of primary consideration was the

---

[2]Loss, *op. cit.*, p. 18.
[3]V. Geiger-Jones, 242 U.S. 339 quoted in J. K. Lasser and J. A. Gerardi, *Federal Securities Act Procedures* (New York: McGraw-Hill Book Co., 1934), p. 2.
[4]*Ibid.*

interstate nature of the U.S. economic system. The absence of legislation in some states and inadequate laws in others allowed fraudulent practices to continue in spite of regulatory efforts. A study submitted by the Department of Commerce in 1933 indicated that, "The most effective and widely used method of evading the provision of state blue-sky laws consists of operating across state lines."[5]

Another reason for inadequacy of state laws was the seeming reluctance on the part of state legislatures to provide proper enforcement of the laws they had established. State legislatures seemed to be more concerned about having a law on the books than in enforcing proper regulation of securities sales.

Exemptions contained in the blue-sky laws were additional inadequacies of state legislation. Complicating state enforcement was the nearly universal willingness of victims to condone the offense or to accept a compromise. If a state began preparing evidence against a corporation, the company would pay investors for a part of the loss and the state would lose its witnesses and the case.

**Abuses of the 1920s.** The securities market activities of the 1920s are legend. While trading and investment were brisk, the underlying strength of the market was eroding as a result of certain common practices.[6] The first was price manipulation. It was not uncommon for brokers or dealers to indulge in wash sales or matched orders where successive buy and sell orders created a false impression of activity and forced prices up, allowing those involved to reap huge profits before the price fell back to its true market level. Outright deceit by issuing false and misleading statements was another popular manipulative device. All of these manipulative procedures had as their objective the making of profits at the expense of unwary investors. Another practice undermining securities markets was the excessive use of credit to finance speculative activities or to buy stocks on margin. There was no limit to the amount of credit a broker could extend to a customer. As a result, a slight decline in market prices started chain reactions which gained momentum when an overex-

[5]U.S. Department of Commerce, *A Study of the Economic and Legal Aspects of the Proposed Federal Securities Act*, Hearings before House Committee on Interstate and Foreign Commerce on H.R. 4314, 73d Congress, 1st Session, 1933, p. 87.

[6]Securities and Exchange Commission, *25th Annual Report*, 1959, pp. XV–XVIL. The Foreword to this report is obviously an attempt to support the SEC, but it does provide valuable information about the background of the SEC.

tended customer sold out because a margin could not be covered. Such a situation became critical when the market began to decline late in 1929 and early in 1930. The misuse of corporate information by corporate officials and other "insiders" was a fourth practice that led to instability in the securities markets. While positioning themselves to take advantage of fluctuations in stock prices when the news became public, executive officers often withheld information about corporate activities.

Edward R. Willet has described the situation:

> The public outcry arising from the great decline in stocks prices between 1929 and 1933 motivated the passage of the major federal laws regulating the securities industry. During the late 1920's investors speculated excessively. About 55 percent of all personal savings were used to purchase securities and the public was severely affected when the Dow Jones Industrial Average fell 89 percent between 1929 and 1933.

> During this period, security price manipulation was common and satisfactory information concerning securities usually was not available. Regulation was badly needed. It is fortunate that legislation passed during such a period of strong reaction against the industry seems to have been basically good legislation.[7]

**Awakening to the Need.** As state laws proved ineffective, government officials became concerned that "a supplemental Federal law was needed to stop this gap through which were being wasted hundreds of millions of public savings that might otherwise have been diverted to substantial industrial development."[8] The aggregate value of all stocks listed on the New York Stock Exchange was $89 billion before the market began to decline in the fall of 1929. In September and October, the aggregate value dropped by $18 billion. After those two disastrous months, it appeared for a short time that a recovery was under way, but the market softened in the spring of 1930, and a bear market prevailed over the next two and one-half years. In 1932, the aggregate value of stocks was only $15 billion — a drop of $74 billion from 1929.

The transition from state to federal regulation would not be without contest, however, or without a traumatic awakening to the need for federal legislation. As Loss pointed out, "Whether any legislation

[7]Edward R. Willet, *Fundamentals of Securities Markets* (New York: Appleton-Century-Crofts, 1968), p. 211.
[8]Lasser and Gerardi, *op. cit.*, p. 4.

could prevent another such catastrophe is beside the point; it is a simple fact that the developments of 1929–1932 brought the long movement for Federal securities regulation to a head."[9]

**Federal Action.** In March, 1932, the Senate passed a resolution allowing the Banking and Currency Committee to investigate the securities industry. The subsequent far-reaching investigation uncovered a variety of evils. A report to the House of Representatives highlighted the extent of losses incurred by the investing public due to the practices of issuers and brokers:

> During the postwar decade some 50 billions of new securities were floated in the United States. Fully half or $25,000,000,000 worth of securities floated during this period have been proved to be worthless. These cold figures spell tragedy in the lives of thousands of individuals who invested their life savings, accumulated after years of effort, in these worthless securities. The flotation of such a mass of essentially fraudulent securities was made possible because of the complete abandonment by many underwriters and dealers in securities of those standards of fair, honest, and prudent dealing that should be basic to the encouragement of investment in any enterprise.
>
> Alluring promises of easy wealth were freely made with little or no attempt to bring to the investor's attention those facts essential to estimating the worth of any security. High pressure salesmanship rather than careful counsel was the rule in this most dangerous of enterprises.
>
> Equally significant with these countless individual tragedies is the wastage that this irresponsible selling of securities has caused to industry.[10]

Several philosophies prevailed as Congress approached the task of federal legislation. Many advocated a fraud law patterned after New York's Martin Act. These protagonists saw preventive laws as unworkable, unenforceable hindrances to honest business. Those at the other extreme wanted laws patterned after those of several other states that required securities registration and strict qualification. A compromise group spoke for disclosure laws similar to the English Companies Act of 1900.[11]

[9]Loss, *op. cit.*, p. 75.
[10]*Federal Supervision of Traffic in Investment Securities in Interstate Commerce*, H. R. Report No. 85, 73d Congress, 1st Session, 1933.
[11]Loss, *op. cit.*, pp. 76–77.

With disclosure being the main concern, Congress sought securities regulation that would blend the various philosophies. The results were the Securities Act of 1933 and the Securities Exchange Act of 1934. It was under the authority of the latter act that the Securities and Exchange Commission was created. The SEC was given the duty to ensure "full and fair" disclosure of all material facts concerning securities offered for public investment. The Commission's intent is not necessarily to prevent speculative securities from entering the market, but to insist that investors be provided with adequate information. Initiation of litigation in cases of fraud and providing for the proper registration of securities are two supplemental purposes of the SEC.

**Growth of the SEC.** The SEC has experienced an interesting life cycle. The infancy and puberty of the Commission extended to 1945 and were characterized by working out kinks in legislation and establishing the administrative procedures necessary for the new agency. Early commissioners had to be as much salespeople as interpretative geniuses; they inspired confidence in the laws and at the same time enforced them. By 1945, the SEC began to reach maturity. Then for approximately the next 15 years, the Commission concentrated on performing the function assigned by the laws as interpreted in previous years. This period was characterized by very little significant legislation or innovations. Some wider dissemination of information and greater disclosure resulted during this period, but they were only extensions of previous laws. In general, the post-World War II years were marked by public confidence in the securities industry.

A market break in May of 1962 stopped three years of speculative frenzy in glamour stocks and started a new round of legislative inquiry into the adequacy of existing securities legislation. A revitalization of the SEC began, culminating in significant legislation in the 1964 Amendments to the Exchange Act. The 1960s also witnessed a growth of litigation resulting from Section 11 of the 1933 Act. In 1970, several years of investigation of investment companies resulted in amendments to the Investment Company Act of 1940.

The future of securities markets in general will be influenced greatly by the SEC. Investigations of the 1960s have led to some dissatisfaction over the structure of the markets, and the 70s will likely bring efforts to centralize the securities markets with component parts. Other important probable considerations in this decade include negotiated commission rates, the influence of large institutional investors, the role of brokers and dealers, the monopoly of the New York Stock Exchange, and the role of smaller exchanges.[12] Whatever the outcome of these issues, the Commission will, no doubt, be an influential partner in corporate financing procedures in future years.

## ORGANIZATIONAL STRUCTURE OF THE SEC

With this historical background in mind, a closer look at the SEC can now be taken. The SEC is directed by five commissioners, no more than three of whom may be from the same political party. Members of the Commission are appointed by the President of the United States with the approval of the Senate. Each commissioner is appointed for a five-year term with one member's term expiring on June 5 of each year. The President designates one member as the chairman.

The SEC is administered from its Washington, D.C., headquarters and has regional and branch offices in the major financial centers of the U.S. The organizational structure is illustrated by Exhibit 1-1; the regions of the SEC are shown in Exhibit 1-2. The Commission is assisted by a staff of professionals including accountants, engineers, examiners, lawyers, and securities analysts. These professionals are assigned to the various divisions and offices, including the regional offices, shown in the organization chart.

### SEC Divisions

A brief look at the duties of the five divisions and several of the principal offices is appropriate at this point.

**Division of Corporation Finance.** The Division of Corporation Finance is perhaps the most important division for business people and accountants. the division's major responsibilities include: assisting the Commission in establishing and requiring adherence to standards of economic and financial reporting and disclosure by all companies under SEC jurisdiction; setting standards for the disclosure requirements of proxy solicitations; and administering disclosure requirements for the Securities Act, the Securities Exchange Act, the

---

[12]Harold S. Bloomenthal, *Securities and Federal Corporate Law* (New York: Clark Boardman Co., 1972), pp. 1–7 to 1–13. An excellent survey of the life cycle of the SEC.

*Exhibit 1-1*

## Organization Chart of the Securities and Exchange Commission

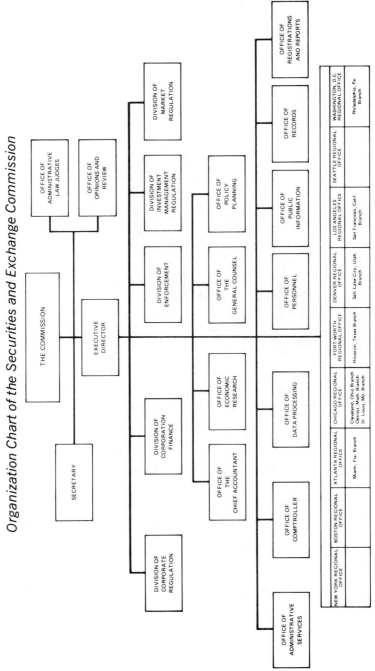

Source: Securities and Exchange Commission, *The Work of the Securities and Exchange Commission* (Washington: U.S. Government Printing Office, 1974).

*Exhibit 1-2*

*Regions of the Securities and Exchange Commission*

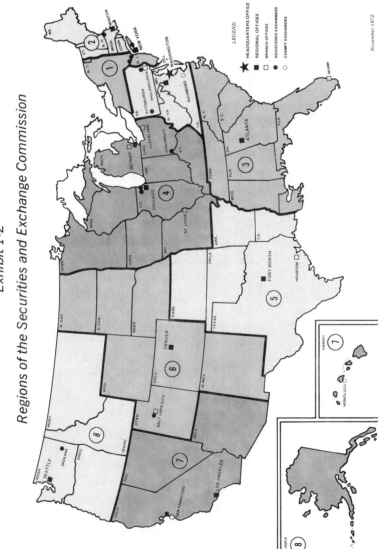

Source: Securities and Exchange Commission, *The Work of the Securities and Exchange Commission* (Washington: U.S. Government Printing Office, 1974).

Public Utility Holding Company Act, and the Investment Company Act. (Each act will be explained in Chapter 2.)

The Division of Corporation Finance reviews all registration statements (lengthy and often complicated narrations of corporate operations), prospectuses, quarterly and annual reports, proxy statements, and sales literature. As these reporting devices are explained later in the book, the reader will better understand the significant influence of this division. Investigations, examinations, formal hearings, and informal conferences are used in the analysis and review of the myriad reports handled each year by this division.

In addition to its review function, the Division of Corporation Finance also provides a useful interpretive and advisory service to help clarify to issuers, accountants, lawyers, and underwriters the application and requirements of the securities laws it administers. Inasmuch as substantially all of the financial statements submitted for review must be certified by independent accountants, a significant portion of an accountant's work with the SEC will be reviewed by this division. The advisory service has proved effective in avoiding problems by providing instructive guidance concerning registration and reporting procedures.

**Division of Market Regulation.** The Division of Market Regulation assists the Commission in the regulation of national securities exchanges and of brokers and dealers registered under the Investment Advisers Act. This division cooperates with the regional offices in investigating and inspecting exchanges, brokers, and dealers. An active and ongoing surveillance of trading markets, both exchanges and over-the-counter markets, is the means by which the Division of Market Regulation exerts its influence and discharges its responsibility. The objective of the surveillance is two-fold. First, the division attempts to discourage manipulation or fraud in connection with sale or purchase of securities. Second, the division supervises the issuance of new securities and ensures adherence to rules regarding the stabilization of securities prices. Because the Commission has the power to suspend an exchange for up to one year, the activities of this division are important and powerful.

The Division of Market Regulation also supervises the broker-dealer inspection program. Brokers and dealers are required to register with the SEC and to submit periodic inspections of their activities. The periodic reports submitted by brokers-dealers are analyzed by this division to ensure proper disclosure and to foster proper conduct by these dealers. Capable of exerting considerable control over the activities of brokers and dealers, the Commission can, and does, disbar brokers-dealers permanently or, as is usually the case, suspend them for a shorter period of time. Not only does it supervise, it also provides interpretive advice to investors and registrants on the requirements of the statutes it administers. The counselor role has proved effective in avoiding possible problems, thus making the remainder of this division's work easier.

**Division of Enforcement.** The Division of Enforcement is responsible for the review and direction of all enforcement activities of the regional offices, supervision of investigations conducted pursuant to federal securities laws, and institution of injunctive actions and determination concerning whether available evidence supports allegations in complaints. Since it is responsible for reviewing cases sent to the Department of Justice for criminal prosecution, this division maintains close cooperation with the Office of the General Counsel.

**Division of Corporate Regulation.** The Division of Corporate Regulation has two major responsibilities. The first is to help administer the Public Utility Holding Company Act of 1935; the second is to perform the Commission's advisory functions to U.S. district courts under Chapter X of the Bankruptcy Act for corporations having numerous private stockholders.

The essence of the Public Utility Holding Company Act of 1935 is the requirement that large utilities be physically integrated and regulated to prevent unnecessary complexities in corporate structure. The principal regulatory provision of the Public Utility Holding Company Act gives the SEC power to regulate securities issuances, sales and purchases of securities by utilities, and the interest in other businesses by utilities. Accounting functions and business transactions with affiliates are also regulated by the SEC. To illustrate the extensive work done by the Commission under the Public Utility Holding Company Act of 1935, more securities releases, official pronouncements of policy and procedures, have been given pursuant to the 1935 Act than under any other federal securities law. The Division of Corporate Regulation is responsible for this effort.

Chapter X of the Bankruptcy Act allows the SEC to act as a disinterested adviser to federal courts in proceedings involving the reorganization of companies with financial difficulties. In conjunction with regional offices, the Division of Corporate Regulation assists the SEC in determining the extent of participation in some proceedings and deciding the Commission's position in a reorganization. Actual court appearances are usually made by General Counsel, but this division must prepare reports and position papers in support of the Counsel.

**Division of Investment Management Regulation.** The Division of Investment Management Regulation assists the SEC in the administration of the Investment Company Act of 1940 and the Investment Advisers Act of 1940. All investigations and inspections arising from these acts and matters concerning the services provided by investment companies and dealers are responsibilities of this division. Reporting and enforcement requirements are the responsibilities of other divisions, however.

The reader will probably already have noted that some divisions have overlapping authority. Cooperation between such divisions is essential if the SEC is to function smoothly. The accounting practitioner and the business executive must be aware of the duplications in order to successfully comply with securities statutes. Compliance with one division's requirements does not automatically ensure adherence to another division's statutes.

## Major Offices

For the purposes of this book, an introduction to the principal offices functioning under the Commission is necessary. The numerous regional offices serve as field representatives for the administration and enforcement of federal securities legislation. They serve as the eyes and ears of the Commission as these offices have considerable power to initiate investigations into possible violations of securities laws, while working in connection with the five divisions. The *Federal Securities Law Reporter* lists ten functions of regional offices, and seven have to do with investigating powers and authority. The other three functions are related to advisory roles under different acts.[13]

[13]*Federal Securities Law Reporter* (New York: Commerce Clearing House). Pages 1042 to 1052 of Vol. 1 give an excellent description of the organizations of the SEC listing all divisions and offices. Andrew Downey Orrick has given a thorough study of divisional responsibilities in "Organization, Procedures and Practices of the Securities and Exchange Commission," *George Washington Law Review*, Vol. 28. No. 1 (October, 1959). The organization has changed somewhat since Orrick's article, but it still serves as an excellent source.

A major part of the investigative activities conducted by regional offices is concerned with brokers and dealers. All registered dealers are subject to surprise inspections to ensure compliance with statutory provisions related especially to accounting procedures. Accountants serving a broker or dealer should be fully aware of accounting policies related to their client's business.

**Office of the Chief Accountant.** The Office of the Chief Accountant provides the Commission with expert advice in matters of accounting and auditing. The goal of the Chief Accountant is the upgrading of accounting and auditing standards that will provide the disclosure the Commission seeks. The SEC has been given statutory power to develop accounting principles, and the Chief Accountant is primarily responsible. He directs the development of administrative policy concerning accounting matters and the preparation of accounting rules and regulations. The Chief Accountant also maintains a liaison with representatives of the American Institute of Certified Public Accountants (AICPA), the Financial Accounting Standards Board (FASB), and others who are engaged in the development of accounting principles. (Chapter 5 focuses attention on the interaction between the SEC and the accounting profession in the development of generally accepted accounting principles.)

**Office of the General Counsel.** The Office of the General Counsel is the chief legal office of the Commission. The responsibilities of this office are three-fold:

1. to represent the Commission in judicial proceedings;
2. to handle legal matters which cut across the lines of work of several operating divisions;
3. to provide advice and assistance to the Commission, its operating divisions, and regional offices with respect to statutory interpretation, rule making, legislative matters, and other legal problems. ...[14]

In the execution of these responsibilities, General Counsel can act on its own initiative as well as at the request of the Commission. The office helps prepare reports to Congress and coordinates the preparation of any legislative proposals offered by the Commission. It also reviews all cases where criminal prosecution is recommended.

[14]Securities and Exchange Commission, *The Work of the Securities and Exchange Commission* (Washington: U.S. Government Printing Office, 1974), p. 20.

**Other Offices.** Other offices provide vital support for SEC activities, but their work exceeds the scope of this book. The serious student can find descriptive material in SEC publications.

## SUMMARY

A popular misconception is that federal securities laws resulted from the market crash and ensuing depression of the 1930s. It is true that final impetus was given to federal laws by these events, but attempts at federal control and supervision of securities markets extends to the late 19th century in this country and back as far as the 13th century in England.

Inasmuch as public financing is essential to the U.S. economy, investor confidence in securities is imperative. When confidence was shaken during the depression, restoration of public confidence was viewed as holding the key to economic recovery. The Securities Act of 1933 and Securities Exchange Act of 1934, along with other statutes, were attempts to infuse a new spirit of trust in securities while protecting the public from fraudulent losses. Disclosure of pertinent information, coupled with the power to enforce the law against fraudulent acts, became the primary objective of the newly created SEC.

The SEC is organized in a manner conducive to authoritative supervision, allowing honest trading in investment securities, while prohibiting deceit and manipulation. To enable the SEC to accomplish its purpose, five major operating divisions were established. The divisions are organized along functional lines with each division having responsibilities under one or more of the Securities Acts. Assisting these divisions are several staff offices that lend specific, professional expertise to each of the operating divisions. Regional and branch offices are involved in the investigative activities of the Commission, but they also provide an effective network of receiving and disseminating important information.

A closer look at the laws administered by the SEC comprises the next chapter.

## Discussion Questions

1. How did businesses evolve into a state where external disclosure of financial information became necessary?

2. Was securities legislation in the 1930s the first attempt at regulation of capital markets?

3. What are blue-sky laws? Explain the major categories of these laws. Have they been effective in regulating securities? Why or why not?

4. List the practices during the 1920s that led to the erosion of the stock market. Explain why those practices had such a negative effect.

5. What is the primary function of the SEC? Explain.

6. What degree of influence does the SEC have in the securities markets? What role do you see the SEC taking in relation to the securities markets during the next decade?

7. Describe the general characteristics of the organization of the SEC. Identify each of the divisions and explain the major purpose and function of each.

8. Explain the activities and the importance of the regional offices.

9. What is the role of the Chief Accountant? Why is this role so important to the accounting profession?

# Chapter *2*   LEGAL FRAMEWORK OF THE SEC

Since the SEC functions with the authority of law, attention must be given to the acts constituting the legal basis from which the Commission operates. Chapter 2 presents a brief introduction of each of the several acts involved to give the reader an appreciation for the scope of authority of the SEC. While the chapter does not provide great detail, sufficient exposure is given so that the salient portions of each act can be properly examined and explained.

This exposure is important to the accountant and business executive since each has a vital role, both statutory and assumed, under several of the acts. Further, the past several years have seen a proliferation of securities available to investors, each issue being supported by extensive financial reports, many of which are certified by public accountants. As the number of securities issued and traded has increased, accountants and businesspeople have played an important role in the securities market. Furthermore, expanding SEC reporting requirements demand the constant attention of accountants and businesspeople. Students of accounting and business must, therefore, be aware of the basic laws governing the SEC and of the empowering acts of the SEC. An overview of the registration process will be deferred to Chapter 3, making these two chapters of real importance to the business student.

A recent statement by the SEC sums up the stated purpose of the Commission — to provide "full and fair" disclosure to investors.

Congress, in enacting the Federal Securities laws, created a continuous disclosure system designed to protect investors and to assure the maintenance of fair and honest securities markets. The Commission, in administering and implementing these laws, has sought to coordinate and integrate this disclosure system. . . . The legislative history of the Securities Act of 1933 indicates that the main concern of Congress was to provide full and fair disclosure in connection with the offer and sale of securities.[1]

The acts also give the Commission the authority to regulate problem areas in the economy in the interest of consumers in general.

## PRIMARY ACTS

The primary acts administered by the SEC are the Securities Act of 1933 and the Securities Exchange Act of 1934. Both acts have been revised through amendments, and the emphasis on disclosure has been increased. The major effort of accounting-related SEC business is controlled by these two acts and by the forms they require.

### Securities Act of 1933

The first of the securities laws passed under Roosevelt's New Deal was the Securities Act of 1933. This act was designed to protect investors from the false claims that had been rampant prior to the stock market crash in 1929. The purpose of the 1933 Act is to regulate the initial offering for sale and the actual sale of securities that use the mail (interstate commerce) for offers or distribution. The 1933 Act does not concern itself with the trading of securities after their initial distribution.

**Objectives of the 1933 Act.** The Securities Act of 1933, often referred to as the "truth in securities" law, has two basic objectives: "(a) to provide investors with material financial and other information concerning securities offered for public sale; and (b) to prohibit misrepresentation, deceit, and other fraudulent acts and practices in the sale of securities generally (whether or not required to be registered)."[2]

[1]The Securities and Exchange Commission, *SEC Docket* (Vol. 4, No. 5, May 7, 1974), p. 155.
[2]The Securities and Exchange Commission, *The Work of the Securities and Exchange Commission* (Washington: U.S. Government Printing Office, 1974), p. 1.

The first objective is an attempt to ensure that the investor is given full and fair disclosure of all pertinent information about a firm. This objective is accomplished by the requirement that any firm offering securities for public sale, except those specifically exempted, must file a registration statement with the Commission and provide the investor with a prospectus that contains most, but not all, of the information given to the SEC. The law assumes, rightly or wrongly, that the disclosure of information concerning the issue and the offering will allow an investor to make an informed choice among alternative investments.

Such stringent registration requirements do not prohibit speculative securities from entering the market, nor do they guarantee against losses; but disclosure allows an investor to examine investment possibilities more carefully.

While it is not the purpose of the 1933 Act or the SEC to judge the merits of securities offered for sale, the SEC, through its strict disclosure and review requirements, has in the past blocked the issuance of very speculative offerings by exhausting the patience of the issuer or by stating that the registration statement or prospectus was deficient. (The type and extent of SEC reviews are explained in Chapter 3.) The intent of the law is that "the Government should not take the responsibility for determining the investor's choice among investment opportunities but should make certain the investor has an opportunity to make such choice on the basis of full disclosure of the pertinent facts and in the absence of fraud."[3]

Registration itself does not guarantee the accuracy of the registration statement or the prospectus. Severe penalties for false or misleading information promote the implementation of the second objective of this Act and encourage the issuer to provide information that is complete, accurate, and honest. The 1933 Act also provides for the right of an investor to recover, through state or federal courts, any losses incurred as a result of false or misleading registrations and prospectuses. Section 11 of the 1933 Act states that anyone connected with the registration statement, including accountants, is liable for the accuracy of the statements. (Chapter 5 discusses the liability of managers and accountants under the various acts.)

As securities have been issued more frequently and in greater quantities, there appears to have been an increase in the number of

[3]Hamer H. Budge, Statement before Subcommittee on Antitrust and Monopoly of Senate Committees on the Judiciary (February 18, 1970). Budge is a former Chairman of the SEC.

court proceedings for fraudulent practices or negligence in the sale of securities. The *Wall Street Journal* and other publications, as well as SEC publications, almost daily contain reference to such actions. Many of the litigations involve the accounting practices of firms which prepare financial statements for an issuer or involve the individuals who have been involved in fraudulent presentations. Fair and full disclosure is the objective, and the SEC insists that companies comply or penalties will be imposed.

Not all securities listed for sale are registered with the Commission. The 1933 Act provides for certain exemptions, namely:

(1) private offerings to a limited number of persons or institutions who have access to the kind of information registration would disclose and who do not propose to redistribute the securities, (2) offerings restricted to the residents of the State in which the issuing company is organized and doing business, (3) securities of municipal, State, Federal and other governmental instrumentalities, of charitable institutions, of banks, and of carriers subject to the Interstate Commerce Act, (4) offerings not in excess of certain specified amounts made in compliance with regulations of the Commission, . . . and (5) offerings of "small business investment companies" made in accordance with rules and regulations of the Commission.[4]

Exemptions are generally divided into two categories: (1) exempt securities, and (2) exempt transactions. Securities exempt are those offered by banks, nonprofit organizations, governments, and common carriers. Exempt transactions are *intrastate* offerings, private offerings (see 1 in above quotation), and transactions of limited size (generally $500,000 or less). It should be noted that these exemptions are from the registration requirements; they do not decrease the liability imposed by the act.

**Effect on Accountants.** Among the most important information contained in a registration statement and prospectus are the financial statements and supporting schedules, most of which must be certified by an independent public accountant. The certification must be a manually signed document accompanying the registration statement. The preparation and auditing of these financial reports in the manner required is a tedious yet important job, and it is the principal work done by accountants under the 1933 Act.

Other work incidental to but not required by the 1933 Act includes the issuance of a comfort letter by an independent accountant.

4The Securities and Exchange Commission, *op. cit.*, p. 2.

The underwriter of an issue has an obligation to exercise "due diligence" to verify the accuracy of the registration statement itself as well as any unaudited, interim statements included to update the certified statements. The "comfort letter," given to the underwriter and legal counsel, gives negative assurance on the unaudited financial statements of the issuer; i.e., states that the reviewing accountant has found no indication that the statements are false or misleading. The accountant does not generally perform an audit of the interim statements. The comfort letter is not a requirement of the 1933 Act or the SEC, but it is generally requested by the underwriter as evidence that due diligence has been exercised concerning the reliability of the prospectus.[5]

Another important function of the accountant is providing assistance in preparing, reviewing, and submitting the financial statements and supporting schedules required in a registration statement. This function is discussed in more detail in the next chapter.

## Securities Exchange Act of 1934

Soon after passing the Securities Act of 1933, Congress moved to regulate the trading of securities on secondary markets through brokers and exchanges and to eliminate certain abuses in the trading of securities after their initial distribution. Congress also realized the necessity of having an organization designed specifically to carry out the function described in the laws it was considering. Thus, it was with the Securities Exchange Act of 1934 that the SEC came into being.

In general, the 1934 Act is a one-act statement of all the authority needed to successfully regulate securities trading on the national exchanges. Unlike the 1933 Act which restricts itself primarily to initial offerings, the 1934 Act is concerned with several aspects of securities trading. The 1934 Act initially extended the full and fair disclosure doctrine to include all companies that had securities registered on the national securities exchanges. In 1964, the Securities Act Amendments extended the disclosure requirement to the securities of companies which trade on over-the-counter markets. This

---

[5]See AICPA Committee on Auditing Procedure, *Statement on Auditing Procedure*, Publication No. 48 (New York, 1971). This statement explains the comfort letter and gives the opinion of the Committee on Auditing Procedures regarding its use, form, and application.

requirement is limited, however, to companies having over $1 million in assets and 500 or more stockholders.

**Registration of Securities Issuers.** Section 12(a) of the 1934 Act states that companies desiring to have their securities traded on any of the national exchanges (now extended to include over-the-counter markets except for the securities of small companies, under the size limitations mentioned above) must file a registration statement quite similar to, although not as extensive as, the one required by the 1933 Act. It must be understood that these two acts are independent, and registration under one does not meet the requirement of the other. A prospectus is not required by the 1934 Act because trading on secondary markets is open to everyone, and companies cannot determine who might be interested in their securities.

In addition to the registration of outstanding securities and the disclosure involved in that process, updated information must be filed with the Commission by means of periodic report forms — the 10-K, 8-K, and 10-Q forms are the most widely known and used. All of this information, with certain limited exceptions, is public information and is available at the offices of the SEC, investment banking firms, and the securities exchanges.

As in the case of the 1933 Act, registration and continued reporting do not guarantee accuracy. However, the SEC can file court proceedings against those who prepare and file (or are associated with the filing of) fraudulent reports and can suspend the trading in securities of companies which fail to make full and accurate reports or which repeatedly fail to file on a timely basis.

**Registration of Exchanges and Brokers.** Another important aspect of the 1934 Act is the requirement that national securities exchanges be registered. In its application for registration, a national exchange must file with the Commission a report giving comprehensive data concerning the rules of the exchange and the scope of its operations. The exchange must also agree to comply with the requirements of the 1934 Act and to enforce compliance by the brokers who are members of the exchange. The application will be approved if the SEC feels the exchange is organized in a manner that will allow it to adhere to the requirements of the law. The disclosures subsequently required of exchanges allow the Commission to monitor their activities continuously.

Brokers dealing in over-the-counter markets are also required to register with the SEC. (Brokers who deal only in intrastate sales are exempt from this registration requirement.) The Commission has specified that registered brokers and dealers must submit periodic reports and records of transactions and has established minimum capital requirements for brokers. An extensive revision of these requirements was made in Accounting Series Release (ASR) No. 156, dated April 26, 1974. This release specifies the ledgers, accounts, and journals that must be kept and the maximum number of days that can elapse between any transaction and the posting or recording of the transaction.

**Protection of Investors.** The 1934 Act contains other measures that are designed to provide fair securities markets for the investor. The law prohibits the use of any "manipulative or deceptive device or contrivance" [Section 10(b)]. The 1934 Act specifically forbids such practices as wash sales and matched orders (where buy and sell orders are made in rapid succession in order to give the impression of active trading), induced trading by false statements, misuse of pro forma financial statements, and certain other practices such as price stabilization and short sales. In general, it discourages any fraudulent plot or scheme designed to manipulate the market for temporary advantage.

To further protect the investor, any officer, director, or person who owns more than 10 percent of a registered company must file an initial report with the SEC as well as the exchange where the company's securities are traded and must list any holdings of equity securities. Thereafter, a report must be filed for any month in which changes are made in the holdings. Any gains made on short-term transactions (less than six months) or on short sales may be recovered by the company or on its behalf by any of its security holders. This requirement discourages an "insider" from using confidential corporate information to advantage in trading equity securities. A considerable amount of litigation has been enacted relating to insider trading, with the insider almost always the loser.

**Other Provisions.** In regulating securities trading on the national exchanges, the 1934 Act has three other important provisions. The first is the authority to regulate proxy solicitation for the election of directors or for approval of other corporate actions. This provision is closely tied to the disclosure objective of the 1934 Act. Section 14(a) gives very broad power to the SEC by making it unlawful for anyone to solicit a proxy or consent except under the rules the SEC may establish for the protection of investors. The purpose of the proxy rule is to ensure that sufficient disclosure is made to permit an investor to use the right to vote intelligently. These proxy requirements are probably the most effective disclosure rules in the area of securities laws.

Another provision is the disclosure of all pertinent information in tender offer solicitations. Before tender offers can be made, the prospective buyer must file with the SEC the following information: the principal business of the buyer, source of funds to be used in the purchase, purpose of the transaction, and the amount of equity securities to be purchased. This regulation prevents any surprise "take-over bids" and allows an issuer time to consider the tender offer.

A final provision of the 1934 Act authorizes the Board of Governors of the Federal Reserve System to control the use of margins in securities trading. Margins can be raised or lowered, depending on whether the Federal Reserve desires to stimulate or to curtail investment. The SEC retains the responsibility of enforcing the credit restrictions, which it does in connection with its periodic review of the exchanges and brokers.

**Enforcement Power.** The SEC is given broad enforcement powers under the 1934 Act. If the rules of operation for exchanges prove to be ineffectual in implementing the requirements of the Commission, the SEC can alter or supplement them. The SEC can suspend trading of a security for not more than 10 days (a series of orders has enabled the SEC to suspend trading for extended periods, however) and can suspend all trading on any exchange for up to 90 days. If substantive hearings show the issuer failed to comply with the requirements of the securities laws, the Commission can delist any security. Brokers and dealers can be prevented, either temporarily or permanently, from working in the securities market; and investigations can be initiated if deemed necessary to determine violations of any of the acts or rules administered by the SEC.

**Effect on Accountants.** Accountants can also be censured, and their work is subject to approval by the SEC. An accountant is involved in the preparation and review of a major portion of the reports and statements required by the 1934 Act. The financial statements in the annual report to stockholders and in the 10-K report must be certified. In addition, accountants consult and assist in the preparation of the periodic 8-K and quarterly 10-Q reports which represent the result of many hours of work by both the accounting staff of the registrant and by its independent certifying accountants.

Since the SEC requires periodic reports from the brokers and dealers who are registered in the over-the-counter markets, a thorough audit of the books of these brokers must be made, and extensive financial reports must be prepared and certified by an independent public accountant. With the new requirements of ASR 156, accountants should be equipped to give expert assistance to a broker to assure that the broker meets the strict record-keeping and financial reporting requirements of the SEC.

In addition to the auditing of brokers' and dealers' books, another important area of concern for the accountant is proxy statements. These statements, for the most part, must be accompanied and supported by certified financial statements. The accountant, again, is expected to provide professional expertise in the proper preparation and documentation of these statements.

## SECONDARY ACTS

As well as the primary acts — the Securities Act of 1933 and the Securities Exchange Act of 1934 — there are secondary acts of importance to businesses and to the public in general. These other acts, in order of discussion, are: The Public Utility Holding Company Act of 1935; the Trust Indenture Act of 1939; the Investment Company Act of 1940; the Investment Advisers Act of 1940; the National Bankruptcy Act, Chapter X; and the Securities Investor Protection Act of 1970.

### Public Utility Holding Company Act of 1935

**Legal Requirements.** The Securities and Exchange Commission stated of the Public Utility Holding Company Act of 1935: "This statute was enacted by Congress to correct the many abuses which congressional inquires had disclosed in financing and operation of electric and gas public utility holding company systems."[6]

In 1928, when the Federal Trade Commission (FTC) began a thorough review of the practices and organizational structure of the utilities industry, it uncovered a system of huge utility empires controlling widely scattered subsidiaries which had little or no economical or functional relationship to each other. Such companies were pyramided

[6]The Securities and Exchange Commission, *op. cit.* p. 12.

together, layer upon layer, and possessed very complex capital structures developed to utilize financial leverage and reduce the equity investment.[7]

As a regulative device given the SEC by the 1935 Act, Section 11, commonly known as the "death sentence," was initiated. The responsibility of the SEC, according to Section 11(a) is "to determine the extent to which the corporate structure . . . may be simplified, unnecessary complexities therein eliminated, voting power fairly and equitably distributed . . . and the properties and business thereof confined to those necessary or appropriate to the operations of an integrated public utility system." The result was a geographic integration of utility companies by which the SEC subdivided nearly all of the utility empires and simplified the capital structure of virtually all utility companies. The goal of the SEC was to create simple, coordinated systems confined to a single area or region, limited in such a way as not to impair the advantages of localized management, efficient operation, and effective local regulation.

The 1935 Act also empowers the SEC to regulate the terms and form of securities issued by utility companies. A reasonable capital structure is thereby maintained and competition is ensured among investment banks for underwriting and other services rendered to utility companies. As a result, the interests of both consumers and investors are protected. Investors benefit from the improved financial stability and strength, and consumers benefit from the regulation of utility company size and operation.

A registration requirement is the primary tool used to correct the abuses found in the exhaustive survey by the FTC. Registration under the 1935 Act requires companies involved in electric utility or retail gas operations to furnish to the SEC information concerning their capital structures and the nature of their businesses. Annual reports are submitted to keep the Commission up-to-date on the activities of registered companies. The 1935 Act also gives the SEC power to regulate the accounting systems of registered companies and requires the SEC to approve any acquisition or disposition of securities and assets and to regulate intercompany transactions, such as loans and dividend payments.

**Effect of Accountants.** Preparation and certification of the financial statements required by this Act are important contributions

[7]*Ibid.*

of the accountant. Reports are required at the time of initial registration; and as a means of having updated information on file at the SEC, they are required each year thereafter. Financial statements prepared according to the detailed instructions of the Uniform System of Accounts for Public Utility Holding Companies and a related system, the Uniform System of Accounts for Mutual Service Companies and Subsidiary Service Companies, require special attention from the accountant. These accounting systems represent the only detailed accounting procedures which have been prescribed by the SEC.

## Trust Indenture Act of 1939

**Legal Requirements.** The Trust Indenture Act of 1939 stipulates that bonds, debentures, and other debt securities offered for public sale can be issued only under a trust indenture approved by the Commission. Because some issuers had failed to provide trustees who were capable of performing adequately on their behalf, the law was passed as protection to purchasers. The act requires a trustee to be an independent corporation (free of conflicting interest) with a minimum capitalization of $150,000. The registration form used under the 1939 Act requires an analysis of the indenture provisions and other information allowing the SEC to rule on the capability of the trustee to serve successfully.

**Effect on Accountants.** There are no requirements for certification of financial data contained in annual reports under this act, but it is desirable to have an accountant review the indenture before it becomes final since it could contain restrictions the accountant needs to understand to serve a firm adequately.

## Investment Company Act of 1940

**Legal Requirements.** The Investment Company Act of 1940 resulted from a comprehensive, four-year investigation of investment companies and investment advisers made by the SEC pursuant to the direction of Congress. The intent of the law is to remedy and control many of the abuses uncovered in the intensive study and to work out a compromise between industry representatives and the SEC. The Commission states the following of this act, which is considered to be the most complex statute administered by the SEC:

Under this Act, the activities and companies engaged primarily in the business of investing, reinvesting, and trading in securities and whose own securities are offered and sold to and held by the investing public, are subject to certain statutory prohibitions and to Commission regulation in accordance with prescribed standards deemed necessary to protect the interests of investors and the public.[8]

Registration with the SEC is required of all companies whose business is described in the foregoing statement. Such registration is very similar to the 1933 and 1934 Acts, but registration under the 1940 Act does not eliminate the requirement for registration under the preceding acts. Additionally, disclosure of the financial condition and investment policies of the company is required; this gives the investor access to complete information concerning the activities of investment companies. All of the disclosures must be updated periodically with reports sent to the SEC.

Other provisions (1) prohibit anyone guilty of security frauds from being associated with investment companies, (2) prohibit transactions between the companies and their directors, officers, or affiliate companies without prior Commission approval, and (3) prohibit pyramids of such companies and cross-ownership of their securities or the issuance of senior securities except under certain conditions.

The investor should not assume that the SEC supervises the investment activities of the companies and should recognize that regulation of a company does not guarantee the securities of that company will be a good investment. Some protection is provided, however, in that reports of company activities, including certified financial statements, must be sent to stockholders at least semiannually.

**Effect on Accountants.** The registration statements and reports of regulated investment companies contain detailed financial statements and schedules, all of which must be certified by independent public accountants who must be elected by stockholders or appointed by directors and ratified by stockholders. The accountant must also conduct periodic, unannounced examinations of the securities held by investment companies and report the result to the SEC. In addition to certifying financial statements, an accountant is required to furnish an opinion covering many of the items in the reports, giving "negative assurance" with respect to some of the items. This opinion is to be given only after an extensive audit has been done to determine the veracity of accounts and procedures.

[8]*Ibid.*, pp. 16–17.

## Investment Advisers Act of 1940

**Legal Requirements.** The Commission states of this act:

This law establishes a pattern of regulation of investment advisers which is similar in many respects to Securities Exchange Act provisions governing the conduct of brokers and dealers. It requires, with certain exceptions, that persons or firms who engage for compensation in the business of advising others about their securities transactions shall register with the Commission and conform their activities to statutory standards designed to protect the interests of investors.[9]

The law is directed towards proper and complete disclosure of information about investment advisers, their backgrounds, business affiliation, and bases for compensation. If the proper disclosure is not made by investment advisers, the Commission has the power either to deny registration or to suspend or revoke existing registration. The SEC may initiate injunctions or recommend prosecution of advisers for willful violations of securities laws. The Commission is also empowered to issue rules defining fraudulent practices which will not be tolerated.

**Effect on Accountants.** While accountants are not required to certify the registration of investment advisers, they may be appropriately involved in preparing and maintaining the extensive records and accounts required by this act. The most important work of accountants under this act is the examination of all securities held by investment advisers on behalf of their clients. Such an examination must be made at least once during each calendar year and must be done without prior notice to the investment adviser. Conforming to the outline prescribed in ASR 103, the result of the examination must be reported to the SEC.

## National Bankruptcy Act, Chapter X

**Legal Requirements.** Chapter X of the National Bankruptcy Act provides for corporate reorganization of financially distressed companies, and the SEC participates as an adviser to the courts during proceedings in which there is substantial public investor interest. The Commission makes recommendations regarding fees, property transactions, interim distribution to security holders, and various

---

[9]*Ibid.*, pp. 17–18.

other legal and financial questions. However, the Commission does not have authority to veto any reorganization plan, to require adoption of its recommendations, or to make decisions in bankruptcy cases.

Of primary importance is the Commission's assistance in the formulation of plans to reorganize debtor corporations. The SEC attempts to recommend reorganization which will maximize the return to the creditors and equity security holders of the corporations.

**Effect on Accountants.** Independent public accountants have no responsibility in any reorganization plan except as they might be serving the interest of the debtor, trustee, or other interested party.

## Securities Investor Protection Act of 1970[10]

**Legal Requirements.** In recent years investors have suffered sizable losses in securities markets due to the failure and financial difficulties of brokers and dealers. Congress enacted the Securities Investor Protection Act of 1970 as an amendment to the Securities Exchange Act of 1934. The 1970 Act created the Securities Investor Protection Corporation (SIPC), a nonprofit organization whose membership comprises the brokers and dealers registered under Section 15(b) of the 1934 Act and members of the national securities exchanges. Five of the seven-member board of directors are appointed by the President of the United States, one by the Secretary of the Treasury, and one by the Federal Reserve Board. Two of the seven members may not be associated with the securities industry.

The SIPC creates a fund by collecting fees from the membership. This fund is used for the protection of investors to a limit of $50,000 for each account and a maximum of $20,000 for cash claims in each account. The Commission can apply to the U.S. District Court for an order compelling the SIPC to protect its customers if the SIPC is lax in this obligation. The SIPC is required to file annual reports and financial statements with the SEC, and the Commission can make inspections of all SIPC activities. Also, the SEC has authority in connection with bylaws and rules of the SIPC.

---

[10]Louis H. Rappaport, *SEC Accounting Practice and Procedure* (3d ed.; New York: Ronald Press Co., 1972), pp. 1.8–1.9.

**Effect on Accountants.** The accountant serves a traditional function by certification of the financial statements of the SIPC. Additionally, the accountant serves as adviser to the SIPC in the maintenance of an adequate accounting system.

## SUMMARY

The reader who has carefully reviewed this survey of laws and acts will be amazed at the broad powers of the SEC to control the activities and to monitor the reports of the majority of business enterprises in the United States. The SEC has been applauded as one of the most effective government agencies for its ability to ensure accurate disclosure of business activity and to control the securities exchange markets in behalf of the investing public. The wide range of the SEC's activities and powers makes it an influential member of the business community.

## Discussion Questions

1. Name the acts governed by the SEC.

2. What are the basic objectives of the Securities Act of 1933? How are these objectives being met?

3. List the major exemptions from registration under the 1933 Act, and list the categories in which they fall.

4. What is a comfort letter? Why is one issued in connection with a registration statement?

5. What did Congress attempt to do by passing the Securities Exchange Act of 1934? What agency was established by this act?

6. List some of the differences in the requirements of the Securities Act of 1933 and the Securities Exchange Act of 1934.

7. Among the measures provided to protect the outside investor there are certain restrictions on insiders. What are these restrictions and what effects are they likely to have?

8. Explain what a proxy is. What are the proxy solicitation requirements?

9. What are the purposes of the regulations covering a tender offer?

10. How does the Federal Reserve Board regulate margins? What significance does this have?

11. What disclosure tools are used under the Public Utility Holding Company Act of 1935?

12. What are the major purposes of the Investment Company Act of 1940 and the Investment Advisers Act of 1940?

Chapter *3*  # SEC REGISTRATION AND REPORTING

In the previous chapter, each of the acts giving the SEC its power was explained. The purpose of this chapter is to examine the process of SEC registration, including some of the reporting requirements involved.

Registration is a detailed, often lengthy process. With adequate disclosure being the main objective, registration requires simultaneous attention in several areas. Many people have seen incredible juggling acts where a performer keeps as many as seven or eight objects flying in the air by using hands, head, mouth, arms, and legs. Similarly, the registration process requires a company's management to coordinate several tasks simultaneously. Some companies are adept and successful at making registration a smooth process, while others drop one or two items, and registration becomes a nightmare of starts and stops.

Registration is a major part of all six of the acts administered by the SEC. With some variation due to the differing purposes of the acts, the process under each act is quite similar in terms of disclosure requirements and procedures. In review, the various acts and their respective general registration requirements are:

(1) Securities Act of 1933: Registration of new securities offered for public sale.
(2) Securities Exchange Act of 1934: Continuous reporting of publicly owned companies and registration of securities, security exchanges and certain brokers and dealers.

(3) Public Utility Holding Company Act of 1935: Registration of interstate holding companies covered by this law.
(4) Trust Indenture Act of 1939: Registration of trust indenture documents and supporting data.
(5) Investment Company Act of 1940: Registration of investment companies.
(6) Investment Advisers Act of 1940: Registration of investment advisers.[1]

The focus of this chapter will be upon registration under the 1933 and 1934 Acts, the most common forms of registration involving businesspeople and accountants. (Additional specific procedures for registration under other acts can be found by reference to the individual acts.)

## THE REGISTRATION PROCESS: AN OVERVIEW

The rapid growth in business activity in the United States has brought a concurrent increase in the need for companies to seek capital to finance their expansion. Much of this capital is obtained from public investment. A look at the registration filings over a recent ten-year period for the 1933 Act alone gives an impressive picture of the magnitude of the work done by the SEC.[2]

| Fiscal Year Ended June 30 | Number of Filings | Dollar Amount (billions) | Percent of Companies Filing for First Time |
|---|---|---|---|
| 1963 | 1,159 | $14.7 | 31% |
| 1964 | 1,192 | 18.6 | 27 |
| 1965 | 1,376 | 19.1 | 33 |
| 1966 | 1,697 | 31.1 | 25 |
| 1967 | 1,836 | 36.2 | 24 |
| 1968 | 2,906 | 54.0 | 34 |
| 1969 | 4,706 | 86.9 | 50 |
| 1970 | 4,314 | 67.0 | 48 |
| 1971 | 3,404 | 70.0 | 29 |
| 1972 | 4,112 | 70.0 | 33 |
| 1973 | 3,744 | 63.0 | 35 |

[1]Leroy G. Ainsworth and Johnny S. Turner, Jr. *An Overview of the SEC with a Guide to Researching Accounting-Related SEC Problems* (Provo: Brigham Young University Press, 1971), p. 11.
[2]Data compiled from SEC Annual Reports to Congress.

Each filing is accompanied by a myriad of documents and schedules and proceeds through the labyrinth explained in this chapter. If the reader keeps these figures in mind as the registration and review procedures unfold, a new appreciation for the task of the SEC will surely result.

In brief, the registration process consists of developing and filing a registration statement with the SEC. A registration statement is generally comprised of two parts, the first part containing information usually included in a prospectus. The prospectus is a rather complete booklet containing information about the company, its history, business, and the financial statements. The prospectus, described in more detail later, includes all information to be presented to prospective investors, and a copy of the prospectus is customarily submitted in full satisfaction of the requirements of the first part. Other detailed information not included in a prospectus would be filed in the second part of the registration statement.

## The Prefiling Conference

In view of the numerous registration statements submitted for review, the SEC staff is available for prefiling conferences with companies having questions about registration. Such conferences often avoid lengthy delays once the registration procedure has begun. In 1948 the Commission stated:

> All members of the Commission's accounting staff are available to advise prospective registrants and their accountants in conference or by correspondence, prior to filing. Experienced practitioners who recognize unique problems regularly follow this procedure and save valuable time for themselves and their clients. The public accountant without experience with the Commission should not hesitate to do likewise.[3]

Recently, the Commission reiterated its policy and expanded its scope:

> The Commission has a long established policy of holding its staff available for conferences with prospective registrants or their representatives in advance of filing a registration statement. These conferences may be held for the purpose of discussing generally the

[3]*14 SEC Annual Report* (Washington: U.S. Government Printing Office, 1948). Quoted in Louis H. Rappaport, *SEC Accounting Practice and Procedures* (3d ed., New York: Ronald Press Co., 1972), p. 1.17.

problems confronting a registrant in effecting registration or to resolve specific problems of an unusual nature which are sometimes presented by involved or complicated financial transactions . . .[4]

A prefiling conference is usually held with the chief accountant of the division having jurisdiction, but unusual problems have advanced to the Office of the Chief Accountant and even a hearing with members of the Commission. Most inquiries, however, are resolved at the division level since firms use this conference privilege to eliminate many roadblocks that might otherwise delay registration.

## Registration Form Selection

Part of the registration process is the selection of the proper form to be used, and the SEC has designed several registration forms for use under each of the acts. These forms contain no blanks to be filled in as do tax forms, but they are narrative in character, giving general instructions about the items of information to be furnished. Detailed information must be assembled by the companies using the form designed for the type of security being offered as well as the type of company making the offer. Louis H. Rappaport said of this procedure: "The decision as to which form to use for registration in a specific case is usually made by the company in consultation with its counsel. Since the question of which form to use is primarily a legal one, the certifying accountant should not make the decision. . . ."[5]

# REGISTRATION AND REPORTING UNDER THE 1933 ACT

The following pages contain a discussion of the forms used under the 1933 Act and the procedures for review by the SEC.

## Basic Forms

Form S-1 is the most commonly used form under the 1933 Act, but there are more than 20 different forms for various types of companies and special situations. Regardless of the form used, certain information is common to all: (a) nature and history of the issuer's business; (b) its capital structure; (c) a description of any material

---

[4]"Guides for Preparation and Filing of Registration Statements," Securities Act Release No. 4936, December 9, 1968.

[5]Rappaport, *op. cit.*, p. 8.2.

contracts including bonus and profit-sharing arrangements; (d) a description of the securities being registered; (e) salaries and security holdings of officers and directors; (f) details of any underwriting arrangements; (g) an estimate of the net proceeds and the uses to which such proceeds will be put; and (h) detailed financial information, such as a summary of earnings, certified balance sheets, profit and loss statements, and supporting schedules.[6]

The following list of forms is not comprehensive, but it gives the major forms used for registration under the 1933 Act. Numerous additional forms of limited, specific use are supplemental to those listed here. A review of the forms will verify the earlier statement that form selection is often a difficult process. The list is in numerical order and is not grouped according to applicability to different industries.

General Description of Common 1933 Act Forms

| | |
|---|---|
| S-1 | General form for securities of all issuers for which no other form is prescribed, except the form may not be used by foreign governments. |
| S-2 | For commercial and industrial companies in the developmental stage. |
| S-3 | For mining corporations in the promotional stage. |
| S-4 | For closed-end management investment companies registered on Form N-8B-1. |
| S-5 | For open-end management investment companies registered on Form N-8B-1. |
| S-6 | For unit investment trusts registered on Form N-8B-2. |
| S-7 | For securities offered for cash of established companies with proven history of earnings. Sometimes called the "short-form" as it abbreviates the lengthy Form S-1. |
| S-8 | For securities to be offered to employees under stock option plans. |
| S-9 | Simplified short form available to "proven" issuers for nonconvertible fixed-interest debt securities. |
| S-10 | For registration of landowner's royalty interests in gas and oil. No financial statements are required. |
| S-11 | For registration of securities of real estate investment trusts or other companies whose primary business is holding real estate. |
| S-12 | For registration of certain American Depository Receipts issued against outstanding foreign securities. No financial statements are required. |
| S-13 | For registration of voting trust certificates under specific circumstances and requirements. |

[6]*Securities Regulations* (Englewood Cliffs: Prentice-Hall), p. 135, para. 118, dated November 1, 1971.

S-14     For registration of securities acquired in mergers or consolidations which are to be redistributed to the public.

S-16     For registration of securities to be offered on behalf of a person other than the registrant, to holders of convertible securities of an affiliate of the registrant, or to holders of outstanding warrants.

1-A     Form used to notify SEC of issue of securities exempted from registration under Regulation A.

In order to give the reader an idea of the mechanics involved in registration and the review procedures of the Commission, a summary of the process under the 1933 Act is given. Significant differences between the 1933 and 1934 Acts will be described later in this chapter, but the process is essentially the same under any of the acts.

## Preparation of the Registration Statement

The problems of management really begin when the registration statement is being prepared for filing:

> The preparation of a registration statement for filing under the Securities Act of 1933 is almost invariably a combined operation. Representatives of the management of the registering company, the underwriters, the independent public accountants, counsel for the company, counsel for the underwriters, and, occasionally, engineers or appraisers — all have important roles in preparing the registration document.[7]

Compiling all of the information used in registration may well occupy the time of the several people mentioned above for well over a month. Additional time will be needed to draft the information into a statement acceptable to a company's board of directors.

Anywhere from one and a half to three months may be involved in the initial preparation of the statement. The time spent is often necessary to ensure that information is complete and accurate. Harry Heller states:

> It cannot be emphasized too strongly that the accuracy and adequacy of the registration statement is ultimately the responsibility of the company and its directors, officers, underwriters, and the independent public accountants whose audit and certificate in respect of financial statements is required by the statute. . . .[8]

[7]Rappaport, *op. cit.*, p. 7.1.
[8]Harry Heller, "Disclosure Requirements Under Federal Securities Regulations," *The Business Lawyer* (January, 1961), p. 301.

When the document is complete, it must be delivered to the main office of the SEC in Washington, D.C. (A branch office cannot accept a registration statement.) Three complete copies of the statement and all schedules, exhibits, and the prospectus must be submitted at the time of filing. Ten additional copies of the registration statement without the exhibits must be furnished for use by the SEC staff. The required filing fee is "1/50 of 1% of the 'maximum aggregate price' at which the securities are proposed to be offered; the minimum fee is $100."[9]

## SEC Review

The review process begins when the SEC receives a completed registration statement. The statute provides that the registration statement becomes effective 20 days after it is filed. However, the effective date for the registration is usually delayed by the review and amendment procedure.

**Review of the Statement.** A normal examination by the SEC staff consists of a review of the statement and a comparison with other information available about the issuer, the industry, and other companies in the industry. This review is made by the Division of Corporation Finance. A branch chief gives a copy of the registration statement to an analyst, an attorney, and an accountant. The analyst reviews for proper form and other nonfinancial information, while the attorney examines the legal aspects and the accountant reviews the financial statements and schedules. The purpose of this examination is to detect any materially untrue, incomplete, or misleading information.

Memoranda are submitted by each of the three staff experts to the branch chief for review. A "letter of comments," generally known as a "deficiency letter," outlines the deficiencies the staff has found in the registration statement and makes suggestions for improvements in the document. The letter, which is not part of the public record, is sent to the registrant as soon as possible so that amendments or other appropriate action may be taken. The letter of comments does not delay the effective date of the registration, but if corrections cannot be made within 20 days, the SEC usually asks the issuer to file a

[9]*Securities Regulations* (Englewood Cliffs: Prentice-Hall), p. 138, para. 124, dated April 22, 1970.

delaying amendment. The submission of any amendment usually renews the 20-day waiting period.

**Alternatives Available to SEC for Noncompliance.** If a firm does not make an attempt to amend its original document, the SEC has three possible courses of action. The first is to let the statement become effective in a deficient manner, knowing the company will be liable for any actions resulting from misleading information. However, since its goal is to protect the investor, the SEC is generally not willing to let a deficient statement become effective. Furthermore, companies would rather not be the object of lawsuits for their own deficiencies.

The second action the SEC can take is to issue a refusal order. In a refusal order, the SEC must notify an issuer of defects within ten days after the filing date and a hearing must be held sometime during the next ten days to allow for correction. Because of the time pressures and lags involved, this action has been used sparingly by the SEC.

The final course of action is issuance of a stop order. A stop order can be issued either before or after the effective date, and it halts further consideration of the statement (if before the effective date) or stops further trading of the security (if after the effective date). As cited in the *Securities Regulations*, such drastic action is generally not needed since most firms reply quickly to the deficiency letter.

> In effect, because of the weapons outlined above, the SEC has been able to use the letter of comments to compel correction of the registration statement. In only rare instances has the SEC had to resort to the stop order; these have been mainly in cases of flagrant violations.[10]

**Types of Review Procedures.** As explained earlier, the number of filings under the 1933 Act has greatly increased in recent years. The SEC attempted to respond to the greater workload by streamlining the lengthy review process just outlined. In 1968, the Division of Corporation Finance adopted a new procedure for review of registration statements. These procedures were reaffirmed in 1972 by Securities Act Release No. 5231. The Division was given the latitude of selecting from four different review procedures. The type of review to be made is based on an initial evaluation of the registration statement by the Commission staff. The four review procedures are:

[10]*Ibid.*, p. 144, para. 130, dated April 2, 1970.

(1) *Deferred Review:* Invoked when the registration document is so poorly prepared or presents such serious problems that further staff time is not justified. Detailed comments are not prepared, but the registrant is notified of the responsibility to proceed, withdraw, or amend. Appropriate action is recommended by the staff to the Commission if the registrant decides to proceed without taking corrective measures.

(2) *Cursory Review:* Registrant is advised that only a cursory review of the statement has been made by the staff and no comments will be made. The issuer will be asked to provide letters from its chief executive officer, independent auditors, and managing underwriter, stating that all are aware of the review made and of their statutory responsibilities under the 1933 Act. Upon receipt of such letters, the staff recommends that the statement become effective.

(3) *Summary Review:* Registrant is advised that a limited review has been made of the registration statement and only comments that arise from that review are submitted to the registrant for consideration. Supplemental letters from the same individuals mentioned in the "Cursory Review" are requested containing similar declarations. Upon receipt of the assurances and satisfactory compliance with the staff's limited comments, the statement will be declared effective.

(4) *Customary Review:* The more complete accounting, financial, and legal review explained earlier is given to many registration documents.[11]

Regardless of the type of review, the burden of adequate disclosure is placed squarely on the shoulders of company management who must assume liability for what is published in its name.

## The Waiting Period

An important feature in the Securities Act of 1933 is the provision for the 20-day waiting period between filing and the date the registration becomes effective. This process can be accelerated, but with the rapid increase in number of registrations, there has been no "normal" waiting period — the effective date is almost always delayed. In 1962, when there were numerous first-time registrants, it took nearly three months between filing and receipt of the letter of comments. In 1965, it took only ten days for some registrations to be processed. The range is skewed to the longer time, however, which makes it even more necessary that a statement be adequately prepared. Then a company can move rapidly into a constantly changing securities environment.

[11]The review procedures are explained in more detail in Rappaport, *op. cit*, pp. 7.5–7.6.

**Indication of Interest.** A company need not sit idle during the waiting period; it can move to make an announcement of the prospective issue of securities. This can only be an announcement, however, with no solicitation to buy. The *Securities Regulations* states:

> In other words, during the waiting period, dealers may solicit "indications of interest" from their customers, and underwriters may solicit "indications of interest" from dealers. But the dealers cannot enter into contracts of sale, and the underwriters cannot form a selling group of dealers.[12]

An indication of interest expresses possible future intent, but it does not obligate an interested party to consummate the transaction. Under a 1954 amendment, information generally is distributed in three ways: (1) an oral communication; (2) a preliminary, or "red herring" prospectus; or (3) a "tombstone ad."

Word of mouth from an underwriter or dealer to known large investors can prove to be beneficial in stimulating investor interest in a forthcoming security issue. While oral communication may be effective for creating enthusiasm, its effects are probably not as widespread as with the other two methods.

A preliminary prospectus takes the form of the final prospectus in that investment information must be disclosed, but information as to the offering price, commissions to dealers, and other matters related to price are omitted. The name "red herring" is derived from the caption "Preliminary Prospectus" stamped in red ink across the front page. The following statement is also required to be included in print at least as prominent as that in the text of the document:

> A registration statement relating to these securities has been filed with the Securities and Exchange Commission but has not yet become effective. Information contained herein is subject to completion or amendment. These securities may not be sold nor may offers to buy be accepted prior to the time the registration statement becomes effective. This prospectus shall not constitute an offer to sell or the solicitation of an offer to buy nor shall there be any sales of these securities in any state in which such offer, solicitation, or sale would be unlawful prior to registration or qualification under the securities laws of any such state.[13]

[12]*Securities Regulations*, (Englewood Cliffs: Prentice-Hall), p. 183, para. 125, dated April 22, 1970.

[13]Securities and Exchange Commission, *General Rules and Regulations Under the Securities Act of 1933* (Washington: U.S. Government Printing Office, 1968), p. 43.

"Tombstone ads" are often seen in the *Wall Street Journal* and other business periodicals. Section 2(10) of the 1933 Act allows a circular or advertisement which lists where a prospectus may be obtained and by whom orders will be executed. The name comes from the form these advertisements generally take. A typical tombstone ad is shown in Exhibit 3-1. The tombstone ad is not a selling document, but it is used to locate potential buyers whose interest will be sufficiently aroused to obtain a prospectus and to make additional inquiry about the securities.

**Other Waiting Period Activities.** During this same waiting period, the company must also be preparing any substantive amendments or delaying amendments required by the SEC to prevent a deficient statement from becoming effective. Time pressures may become intense as management's attention is diffused to the many tasks being performed simultaneously.

Still another matter requires the attention of company management during the waiting period. The 1933 Act requires the managing underwriter to exercise due diligence to help prevent fraud by making careful inquiry into the nature of the security being underwritten. A due diligence meeting is called between representatives of the issuer, counsel for the issuer, independent public accountants, underwriters, counsel for the underwriter, and perhaps other professionals. Information is exchanged concerning the registration statement and final problems are resolved at this meeting.

## Effective Registration Statement

Once the SEC staff determines that all deficiencies have been corrected and that the issuer and underwriters have properly attended to their concurrent responsibilities, the Commission declares the registration statement effective. The issuer and underwriter are then free to proceed with the distribution and sale of the security.

With certain limited exceptions, all of the information compiled as a part of the registration statement is public information and may be inspected in the Public Reference Room of the Commission in Washington, D.C. Copies of all documents may be obtained, and prospectuses covering recent public offerings may be examined at any SEC office.

## Exhibit 3-1

## A Tombstone Ad

*This announcement is neither an offer to sell nor a solicitation of an offer to buy any of these Shares. The offer is made only by the Prospectus.*

*September 25, 1972*

### 250,000 Shares

### ᕲDESERET ᕲPHARMACEUTICAL COMPANY, INC.

**Common Stock**
$ .50 Par Value

### Price $23.50 Per Share

*Copies of the Prospectus may be obtained in any state from only such of the undersigned as may legally offer these Shares in compliance with the securities laws of such State.*

G.H. Walker & Co.
Incorporated

Bosworth, Sullivan & Company
Incorporated

Blyth Eastman Dillon & Co.
Incorporated

Goldman, Sachs & Co.

Smith, Barney & Co.
Incorporated

Wertheim & Co., Inc.

Burnham & Company Inc.

CBLW-Hayden, Stone Inc.

Clark, Dodge & Co.
Incorporated

Robert Fleming
Incorporated

W.E. Hutton & Co.

Kleinwort, Benson
Incorporated

Ladenburg, Thalman & Co. Inc.

R.W. Pressprich & Co.
Incorporated

Shields & Company
Incorporated

C.E. Unterberg, Towbin Co.

Moore & Schley, Cameron & Co.

Note: This exhibit is a simulation, not an exact reproduction of a tombstone ad.

## Summary of Registration Under 1933 Act

This brief overview serves to initiate the reader to the detail and mechanics of registration required by the 1933 Act. As a summary, Exhibit 3-2 presents a hypothetical example of the registration process. Included in the exhibit is a listing of some of the major events which must take place, an indication of the individuals involved, and some idea of the time required for a registration to be developed and become effective. All of the statutes contain similar registration procedures with variation as to content and purpose.

# REGISTRATION AND REPORTING UNDER THE 1934 ACT

The Securities Exchange Act of 1934 was an attempt to bring together in one statute all of the necessary tools to elicit registration from the many participants in the securities market. The continuous reporting required by the 1934 Act is not designed to protect the investor against loss, but to provide "adequate and accurate disclosure of material facts."[14]

## Report Forms

Since registration and reporting under the 1934 Act are broad in coverage, there are ten separate categories of report forms:

1. Forms for registration of national securities exchanges.
2. Forms for reports to be filed by officers, directors, and security holders.
3. Forms for registration of securities on national securities exchanges.
4. Forms for annual and other reports of issuers.
5. Forms for amendments to registration statements and reports to issuers.
6. Forms for registration of brokers and dealers on over-the-counter markets.
7. Forms for reports by certain exchange members, brokers and dealers.
8. Forms for reports to stabilization.
9. Forms for registration and reporting by national securities associations and affiliates.

[14]Securities and Exchange Commission, *The Work of the Securities and Exchange Commission* (Washington: U.S. Government Printing Office, 1974), p. 2.

*Exhibit 3-2*
*Illustrative Example of Registration Process*

| Event | Participants | Agenda | Timetable |
|---|---|---|---|
| Preliminary meeting to discuss issue | President, VP-Finance, independent accountants, underwriters, counsel | Discuss financial needs; introduce and select type of issue to meet needs. | 1 July (Begin) |
| Form selection | Management, counsel | Select appropriate form for use in registration statement. | 3 July ( 3 days) |
| Initial meeting of working group | President, VP-Finance, independent accountants, underwriter, counsel for underwriter, company counsel | Assign specific duties to each person in working group; discuss underwriting problems with this issue; discuss accounting problems with the issue. | 8 July (8 days) |
| Second meeting of working group | Same as for initial meeting | Review work assignments: Prepare presentation to Board of Directors. | 22 July (22 days) |
| Meeting of board of directors | Board of directors, members of working group | Approve proposed issue and increase of debt or equity; Authorize preparation of materials. | 26 July (26 days) |
| Meeting of company counsel with underwriters | Company counsel, counsel for underwriters, underwriters | Discuss underwriting terms and blue sky problems. | 30 July (30 days) |
| Meeting of working group | Members of working group | Review collected material and examine discrepancies. | 6 Aug (37 days) |
| Prefiling conference with SEC staff | Working group members, SEC staff, other experts as needed | Review proposed registration and associated problems: legal, financial, operative. | 9 Aug (40 days) |

| Action | Participants | Description | Date |
|---|---|---|---|
| Additional meetings of working group | Members of working group | Prepare final registration statement and prospectuses. | 12–30 Aug. (61 days) |
| Meeting with board of directors | Board of directors, members of working group | Approve registration statement and prospectuses; discuss related topics and problems. | 6 Sept. (68 days) |
| Meeting of working group | Members of working group | Draft final corrected registration statement. | 10 Sept. (72 days) |
| Filing registration statement with SEC | Company counsel or representative and SEC staff | File registration statement and pay fee. | 12 Sept. (74 days) |
| Distribution of "red herring" prospectus | Underwriters | Publicize offering. | 16 Sept. (78 days) |
| Receipt of letter of comments | Members of working group | Relate deficiencies in registration statement. | 15 Oct. (107 days) |
| Meeting of working group | Members of working group | Correct deficiencies and submit amendments. | 21 Oct. (113 days) |
| "Due diligence" meeting | Management representatives, independent accountants, company counsel, underwriter's counsel, underwriters, other professionals as needed | Exchange final information and discuss pertinent problems relating to underwriting and issue. | 24 Oct. (116 days) |
| Notice of acceptance | SEC staff | Report from SEC staff on acceptance status of amended registration statement. | 28 Oct. (120 days) |
| Statement becomes effective | | | 18 Nov. (141 days) |

10. Forms for reports by market makers and certain other registered broker-dealers in securities traded on national securities exchanges.[15]

## Selection of Forms

Responsibility for proper selection of the forms to be used is incumbent upon the registrant and its counsel. Again to illustrate the numerous forms used, a brief description of the basic forms required for categories three and four above are given along with a list of the schedules of supporting information that must be filed. The numerical forms are for registration while the numerical-alphabetical forms are for the periodic reports associated with such prior registration — i.e., a firm will register using form 10 and then use form 10-K for its annual reports thereafter.

Forms — 1934 Act

| | |
|---|---|
| 10 | For registration of a class of securities for which no other form is specified. |
| 12 | For registration of securities of an issuer who files with another federal agency (e.g., FTC). |
| 14 | For registration of certificates of deposit. |
| 16 | For registration of voting trust certificates. |
| 18 | For registration of securities of foreign governments or political subdivisions. |
| 19 | For permanent registration of American certificates issued against securities of foreign issuers. |
| 20 | For registration of any class of securities issued by foreign private issuers. |
| 25 | For notification of removal from listing of matured or redeemed securities. |
| 26 | For notification of the admission to trading of a substitute or additional class of security. |
| BD | General registration form for all brokers and dealers. |
| 10-K | Annual report for which no other form is prescribed. |
| 11-K | Annual report for employee stock purchase or similar plans. |
| 12-K | Annual reports form for companies using Form 12 for registration. |
| 14-K | Annual report form of issuers of certificates of deposits. |
| 16-K | Annual report form relating to voting trust certificates. |
| 18-K | Annual reports of foreign governments or political subdivisions. |

[15]Securities and Exchange Commission, *General Rules and Regulations Under the Securities Exchange Act of 1934* (Washington: U.S. Government Printing Office, 1970), p. 143.

19-K    Annual report form for issuers of American certificates.
20-K    Annual report form for foreign private issuers.
7-Q     Quarterly reports of real estate investment trusts or of companies whose major business is holding real estate.
10-Q    Quarterly reports containing specified financial information.
8-K     Current report required to be filed within ten days after the close of a month in which any material event occurs.

*Schedules*

I       Marketable securities — other security.
II      Amounts receivable from underwriters, promoters, directors, officers, employees, and principal holders (other than affiliates) of equity securities of the person and its affiliates.
III     Investments in, equity in earnings of, and dividends received from affiliates and other persons.
IV      Indebtedness of affiliates and other persons — not current.
V       Property, plant and equipment.
VI      Accumulated depreciation, depletion and amortization of property.
VII     Intangible assets, deferred research and development expenses, preoperating expenses and similar deferrals.
VIII    Accumulated depreciation and amortization of intangible assets.
IX      Bonds, mortgages and similar debt.
X       Indebtedness to affiliates and other persons — not current.
XI      Guarantees of securities of other issuers.
XII     Valuation and qualifying accounts and reserves.
XIII    Capital shares.
XIV     Warrants or rights.
XV      Other securities.
XVI     Supplementary income statement information.
XVII    Real estate and accumulated depreciation.
XVIII   Mortgage loans on real estate.
XIX     Other investments.

# DIFFERENCES IN REGISTRATION UNDER THE 1933 AND 1934 ACTS

There are two significant differences that need to be highlighted in the registration procedures required under the 1933 and 1934 Acts. The scope of the registration itself is the first such difference. Under the 1933 Act, registration is for a specific security to be issued in a specific amount. The SEC requires a post-effective report on the sale of a new security to verify the amount sold and to cancel any excess above that amount. Under the 1934 Act, however, an entire class of securities is registered with no amount specified. The registration covers the amount of the security outstanding and any additional shares of that class of security that may be issued in the future. Then, without again experiencing the difficulties of registration, a company may issue more securities.

A second significant difference between the two acts is the extensive reporting requirement of the 1934 Act. As securities listed under the 1934 Act are continuously traded over many years, the statute provides for continuous disclosure of company activities through annual, quarterly, and special reports. Forms 10-K for annual reports and 10-Q for quarterly reports are the most widely used. (The general content of a 10-K annual report is described later.) The previous list, although not complete, is indicative of the requirements.

The annual reports are scrutinized by the staff of the SEC to insure a policy of satisfactory financial reporting is practiced by firms registered under the 1934 Act. Only limited material is not made available to the public. Reports are filed at the regional or branch office where the company has its headquarters, and information can be reviewed by the public at these regional and branch offices.

## REGISTRATION
### UNDER OTHER ACTS

Registration requirements are similar for all of the acts supervised and enforced by the SEC. Registrations are reviewed for completeness and deficiencies that must be corrected. Periodic reports are required by every act except the 1933 Act and the Trust Indenture Act of 1939. These reports contain the same basic information and practically all of this information is made public. Specific questions about the unique procedures of each act can be answered by consulting the text of the act itself.

### SUMMARY

A juggler must concentrate on several things at once and must coordinate body movements to perform successfully. The many simultaneous tasks in which a company engages by seeking registration of its securities with the SEC require thorough concentration and the coordination of the activites of several experts. The registration process, as the reader must be aware, is an important undertaking for both a company and the Commission.

The registration goal of corporations is to tap public capital markets for investment funds to stay abreast of the rapidly expanding business activity in the United States. The goal and responsibility of the SEC is to protect investors by requiring full disclosure of an issuer's activities so that investors can reach informed decisions. Goal congruence is obviously not always achieved, but an integrated, cooperative system is approached by the registration and reporting processes described in this chapter. In the next chapter an actual case illustration shows some typical events, the individuals involved, and an illustrative timetable for the registration process.

## Discussion Questions

1. Briefly outline the registration process for the 1933 Act.

2. What is the policy of the SEC with respect to prefiling conferences? How should accountants advise clients to begin the registration process?

3. What information is commonly required in the basic registration forms?

4. Briefly describe the review procedure followed by the SEC staff upon receipt of the registration statement.

5. What is the purpose of a letter of comments?

6. If a registration statement is deficient, what are the courses of action the SEC may take? What are the results of these courses of action?

7. The types of review of the registration statement by the SEC were concisely set forth in 1972. List and explain these review procedures.

8. While waiting for completion of the review, what can a company do in anticipation of approval from the SEC to proceed?

9. What is a "red herring" or a preliminary prospectus? What information does it contain?

10. What is a "tombstone ad?"

11. How do underwriters exercise due diligence under the 1933 Act?

12. What are the primary differences between the requirements under the 1933 and the 1934 Acts?

*Chapter* **4**  # A COMPARATIVE ANALYSIS

The previous chapter has examined both the registration process and the forms used in that process. An appreciation for the extremely heavy workload of business corporations and the SEC divsions can be gained by multiplying the procedures described several thousand times each year. Besides handling over 4,000 new registration statements yearly, the SEC also receives quarterly, annual, and special reports from over 10,000 United States firms. The burden of the SEC is significant.

The purpose of Chapter 4 is to study the registration statements and periodic reports submitted to the SEC and to compare them with corresponding reports submitted to stockholders. An initial narrative on the purpose and scope of the various financial reports will be followed by comparative illustrations based on an actual case filing.

## *REPORTING RESPONSIBILITIES*

The decision to "go public" is of great importance to any firm. Moving from private to public capital financing involves not only a major strategy shift on the part of management, but also a new emphasis on record keeping and reporting. Managements must be willing to share ownership with outsiders and must make the commitment to use the resources necessary so that investors are well informed of corporate activities. If a management is to answer for its stewardship of invested capital as well as provide for a continuation of capital flow from investor to manager, such reporting is vital.

## Annual Reports

A problem arises, however, because there are two different annual reports prepared by managements. One report is sent to the SEC, while a separate report is given to the investor. The annual reports to the SEC are governed strictly in content and form by federal statutes, while managements have had, in the past, nearly free rein in the preparation of their annual report to stockholders.

For years the SEC has urged managements to make the annual report to stockholders reflect more carefully the extensive disclosure requirements of reports sent to the Commission. Due to the variety of people using stockholders' reports, managements generally have been slow to respond to this request. Individuals from top management to labor unions, from housewives to investment analysts, use annual reports to stockholders and rely on their information. The disparity between audiences presents a real problem for managements in the preparation of the annual report, a problem synthesized quite well in the following statement:

> It is not unlike an effort to write for a medical journal an article on advanced techniques in handling compound fractures that is instructive to a practicing physician, and, at the same time, is useful to a Boy Scout working to earn his merit badge in first aid.[1]

A rather simple answer is to structure the annual report to satisfy the average stockholder and let the experts utilize supplemental sources of information, such as the SEC reports. (Remember most SEC reports are available to the public, but usually only investment analysts have taken the time or money to avail themselves of this information.) This solution — indicated later — has not been adopted.

Historically, the Commission has had some influence on the contents of the stockholders' reports, this influence coming in conjunction with the provisions of the Securities Exchange Act of 1934 dealing with proxy statements. If a proxy solicitation is made on behalf of management and concerns an annual meeting where directors are to be elected, the proxy statement must be accompanied by an annual report. Allowing the SEC some control over corporate information sent to stockholders, this annual report must contain certified financial statements and other specific items of disclosure.[2]

---

[1]Donald P. Jones, "Management Freedom in Annual Reports," *Financial Executive*, (August, 1971), p. 24.
[2]See Section 14 of the 1934 Act.

During the last 40 years, in the author's opinion, there has been an improvement in corporate reporting in the United States. Corporate managements and public accountants have made significant contributions in bringing corporate reports up to their present standards, but the SEC and the securities exchanges must also be given some of the credit for promoting needed improvement. To illustrate the improvements, consider the following quotes taken from annual reports. The first is from a 1902 annual report to shareholders.

> The settled plan of the directors has been to withhold all information from stockholders and others that is not called for by the stockholders in a body. So far no request for information has been made in the manner prescribed by the directors . . .[3]

The second quote is from the 1973 annual report to stockholders of a large manufacturing firm. The firm includes in its stockholder's report substantially all of the information in the annual report submitted to the SEC. The company introduces the report by stating:

> This form, filed each year by all publicly owned companies, contains more detailed information than is given in the typical annual report. Our intention in presenting it here is to give all present and prospective shareholders a comprehensive picture of the firm's business and financial condition.[4]

## Additional Disclosure Requirements

The move to disclose more information in the annual reports to stockholders has been prompted by the recent amendments to the rules covering proxy statements (Rules 14a-3, 14c-3, and 14c-7 of 1934 Act). As nearly all corporations use their annual reports with proxy solicitations, the SEC has substantially increased its authority over corporate reporting. The purposes of the recent action are (1) to require disclosure of more meaningful information in the annual reports while giving managements the discretion of format and (2) to improve the dissemination of the more technical 10-K or 12-K reports filed with the SEC.

Essentially, the new disclosure requirements for a company's annual reports after December 10, 1974, are:

(1) audited financial statements for the last two fiscal years;

[3]Quoted in Jones, *op. cit.*, p. 23. See also Louis H. Rappaport, *SEC Accounting Practice and Procedure* (3d ed.; New York: Ronald Press Co., 1972), pp. 3.4–3.5.
[4]Teradyne, Inc., *1973 Annual Report.*

(2) summary of operations for the last five fiscal years and a management analysis thereof;

(3) a brief description of the business;

(4) a line-of-business or product line report for the last five fiscal years;

(5) identification of directors and executive officers with the principal occupation and employer of each;

(6) identification of the principal market in which the securities of the firm are traded;

(7) range of market prices and dividends for each quarter of the two most recent fiscal years.[5]

An additional requirement states that, upon written request, stockholders will be furnished a free copy of the 10-K report. A reasonable charge may be made for copies of any exhibits accompanying the 10-K report.

The new requirements will tend to reduce the differences between annual reports to stockholders and the annual reports filed with the SEC. Investors will be increasingly exposed to technical information in annual reports and will need to become more sophisticated in their abilities to interpret the information provided.

## COMPARISON OF SEC
## AND CORPORATE REPORTS

Attention will now be given to a comparison between corporate reports to stockholders and those filed with the SEC.

### Overview

Of the numerous forms used for reporting to the SEC (see Chapter 3), only the most commonly used forms will be discussed here. To illustrate the use of the forms and how they appear when complete, the reports of Deseret Pharmaceutical Company, Inc., of Sandy, Utah, will serve as a model. The reports provide contrast for purposes of instruction and serve as a useful example of corporate reporting. Because of continuous changes in reporting standards (established by the FASB, CASB, SEC, and other regulatory agencies), the content of these examples will not completely reflect current requirements. However, the general approach is indicative of the type of disclosure presented in the reports.

[5]Securities Exchange Act of 1934, Release No. 11079 (October 31, 1974).

A reminder must also be given: the forms sent to the SEC are mostly narrative reports accompanied by financial statements and schedules. Managements are responsible for the preparation of the reports, and independent public accountants attest to these financial statements. Each form used in reporting to the SEC has varying requirements as to financial data. The most common forms are:

1. Form S-1, used for the majority of registrations pursuant to the 1933 Act.
2. Proxy statement, used in conjunction with proxy solicitation for the periodic meetings of stockholders.
3. Form 10-K, the primary form for yearly reports under the 1934 Act.
4. Form 10-Q, used by all firms to report quarterly operations under the 1934 Act.

In Exhibit 4-1, the financial data and certification requirements of these four forms and the annual report to shareholders are given. This is by no means an exhaustive list of forms and statements, but gives the reader a comparative basis upon which to examine the differences and similarities between commonly used reports.

## Registration Under the 1933 Act

Form S-1 is most commonly used when a firm wishes to register a security for issue in the primary market. The form is divided into two parts. Part I consists of information that is to be included in the prospectus, and Part II is additional information that is submitted as required. Not all items will appear in every registration statement as some items are mutually exclusive (i.e., items 13, 14, 15).

A copy of a complete registration statement would be needed to explain the entire form. An examination of several items of Part I will appropriately illustrate the narrative and tabular nature of Form S-1. Items 1, 2, 3, 9, 13, and 21 will be shown in Exhibits 4-2 through 4-10. Even for these selected items, only a portion of the total is provided.

Item 1 is intended to give a quick look at the distribution, price, and proceeds of the offering, and must appear on the cover page of the prospectus. Exhibit 4-2 shows the form that is to be used.

Item 2 shows the underwriters and the amounts underwritten. Exhibit 4-3 indicates the method in which the information is presented. (Exhibit 4-3 lists only some of the underwriters used.)

*Exhibit 4-1*

| Registrant's Statements | S-1 | | Proxy[1] | | 10-K | | 10-Q[2] | | Annual[3] Report | |
|---|---|---|---|---|---|---|---|---|---|---|
| | Years | Certified | Years | Certified | Years | Certified | Years | Certified | Years | Certified |
| Unconsolidated Balance Sheet[4] | 1 | Yes | not required | | 2 | Yes | not required | | not required | |
| Unconsolidated Income Statement | 3 | Yes | not required | | 2 | Yes | not required | | not required | |
| Unconsolidated Stockholders Equity | 3 | Yes | not required | | 2 | Yes | not required | | not required | |
| Unconsolidated Changes in Financial Position | 3 | Yes | not required | | 2 | Yes | not required | | not required | |
| Consolidated Balance Sheet | 1 | Yes | 1 | Yes | 1 | Yes | current quarter for two years | | 2 | Yes |
| Consolidated Income Statement | 3 | Yes | 3 | Yes | 5 | most recent 3 years | current quarter & year to date 2 | No | 2 | Yes |
| Consolidated Stockholders Equity | 3 | Yes | 3 | Yes | 5 | most recent 3 years | current quarter 2 | No | 2 | Yes |
| Consolidated Changes in Financial Position | 3 | Yes | 3 | Yes | 2 | Yes | year to date 2 | No | 2 | Yes |
| Summary of Operations[5] | 5 | No | 5 | No | 5 | No | not required | | 5 | No |
| Summarized Profit and Loss[6] | not required | | not required | | not required | | interim quarters | No | not required | |

| | | | | | | |
|---|---|---|---|---|---|---|
| Summarized Capitalization and Equity | not required | as appropriate | not required | interim quarters | No | not required |
| Schedules[7] | not required | Schedule XVI only | as appropriate | not required | | not required |

Notes:

1. Proxy statements require financials only when used for mergers, consolidations, acquisitions, or a change in securities issued. A narrative statement, accompanied by the annual report to stockholders, is sufficient for recurring annual stockholders meetings under most circumstances.

2. Securities Act of 1933, Release No. 5549/December 19, 1974, proposed far reaching revisions of the Form 10-Q. While at this date the proposals have not been accepted, it seems likely they will be adopted in the near future. Exhibit 4-1 incorporates the proposed changes. A subsequent release (No. 33-5579) revises the accountant's specified limited review procedures and certification requirements.

3. SEC control over annual reports comes in conjunction with proxy statement requirements. Exchange Act Release #11079 has substantially increased SEC authority over corporate reports.

4. All unconsolidated statements require special attention. For Form S-1 if the registration has 85% of consolidated sales and assets, or the subsidiary is "totally-held" (defined as substantially all equity held by parent but need not be 100%), unconsolidated statements are not needed. For Form 10-K, if the registrant is an operating company (as opposed to a holding company) or the registrant has 75% of consolidated assets and gross revenues, unconsolidated statements are not needed. This is a complex area, and the SEC procedures play an important part in determining when parent consolidated financial statements are included.

5. The Summary must cover at least 5 years, more if clarification is needed. The Summary need not be certified, but most underwriters require certification; and the SEC needs substantial reason when certification is not given. Predominant practice is to include a complete Income Statement which satisfies the requirements for both the Summary of Operations and Consolidated Income Statements.

6. Summarized Profit and Loss and Capitalization and Equity Statements are comparisons of the interim quarters since the fiscal year with the corresponding periods of the preceding year.

7. There are 19 schedules used, but differing circumstances will require different schedules. No one firm would likely have to include all of the schedules in one year. For a list of the schedules refer to Chapter 3.

*Exhibit 4-2*

## Distribution Spread

|  | Price to Public | Underwriting Discounts and Commissions (1) | Proceeds to Company (2) |
|---|---|---|---|
| Per Share | $       23.50 | $     1.50 | $       22.00 |
| Total | $5,875,000 | $375,000 | $5,500,000 |

(1) The Company has agreed to indemnify the Underwriters against certain liabilities, including liabilities under the Securities Act of 1933. See "underwriting."
(2) Before deducting certain expenses estimated at $102,000, to be paid by the Company. (Deseret)

*Exhibit 4-3*

## Underwriting

In the Underwriting Agreement, the Underwriters, represented by G. H. Walker & Co. Incorporated and Bosworth, Sullivan & Company, Inc., have severally agreed, subject to the terms and conditions contained therein, to purchase from Deseret the respective numbers of shares set forth opposite their names below. The Underwriters are committed to take and pay for all such shares, if any are taken.

| Underwriters | Address | Number of Shares to be Purchased |
|---|---|---|
| G. H. Walker & Co. Incorporated .................. | 45 Wall Street New York, New York  10005 | 40,500 |
| Bosworth, Sullivan & Company, Inc. ............... | 660 Seventeenth Street Denver, Colorado  80202 | 40,500 |
| Blyth Eastman Dillon & Co. Incorporated .................. | One Chase Manhattan Plaza New York, New York  10005 | 10,000 |
| Goldman, Sachs & Co. ........ | 55 Broad Street New York, New York  10004 | 10,000 |
| Smith, Barney & Co. Incorporated .................. | 20 Broad Street New York, New York  10005 | 10,000 |
| Wertheim & Co., Inc. .......... | One Chase Manhattan Plaza New York, New York  10005 | 10,000 |
| Burnham and Company ....... | 60 Broad Street New York, New York  10004 | 6,400 |
| CBWL-Hayden, Stone Inc. ... | 767 Fifth Avenue New York, New York  10022 | 6,400 |

## Form S-1

### Part I

1. Distribution Spread
2. Plan of Distribution
3. Use of Proceeds
4. Sales Otherwise than for Cash
5. Capital Structure
6. Summary of Earnings
7. Organization of Registrant
8. Parents of Registrant
9. Description of Business
10. Description of Property
11. Organization Within 5 Years
12. Pending Legal Proceedings
13. Capital Stocks Being Registered
14. Long Term Debt Being Registered
15. Other Securities Being Registered
16. Directors & Executive Officers
17. Remuneration of Directors & Officers
18. Options to Purchase Securities
19. Principal Holders of Securities
20. Interest of Management in Certain Transactions
21. Certified Financial Statements

### Part II

22. Marketing Arrangements
23. Other Expenses of Issuance
24. Relationship with Registrants of Experts Named in Statement
25. Sales to Special Parties
26. Recent Sales of Unregistered Securities
27. Subsidiaries of Registrant
28. Franchises and Concessions
29. Indemnification of Directors and Officers
30. Treatment of Proceeds from Stock Being Registered
31. Financial Statements

The requirement in item 3 provides an example of the frequent use of narrative to supplement numerical information. Exhibit 4-4 illustrates how Deseret proposed to use the proceeds of the offering.

The major portion of any registration statement is a written explanation of the various items included. One of the lengthiest explanations concerns Item 9, the business of a company. An evaluation is made of significant aspects of a company's operations. Deseret began this section with the description shown in Exhibit 4-5. Following this introduction, a comprehensive review of products, marketing research and development, manufacturing, competition, government regulation, and employees is given. Thus a potential investor has an opportunity to evaluate numerous facets of any company's business.

Most investors are interested in the kind of security being offered and want to know the privileges and limitations inherent in the investment. Items 13, 14, and 15, depending on the type of security being registered, give an explanation of the rights and obligations pertaining to the security. As Deseret's issue was common stock, the information in Exhibit 4-6 appeared as a description.

Exposure to the narrative sections has been given to illustrate the wide variety of subjects covered. The financial statements included in Form S-1 have already been introduced by Exhibit 4-1. Deseret Pharmaceutical again provides a typical format. Appropriately introduced and accompanied by explanatory footnotes, Exhibit 4-7 is illustrative of Deseret's Statement of Consolidated Income. Note that Deseret presented information for 5 years even though the statutory requirement is for three years. (Again recognize that this and other examples in Chapter 4 were prepared according to the existing requirements at the time of preparation. Content changes have and will occur, but the general approach is illustrative.) A Consolidated Balance Sheet (Exhibit 4-8), a Statement of Consolidated Stockholders Equity (Exhibit 4-9), and a Statement of Changes in Financial Position (Exhibit 4-10) are also shown.

The process of review and acceptance of a registration statement has already been explained. The reader should now begin to understand why such a lengthy process is involved in the preparation and review of a registration statement. The other forms used for registration under the 1933 Act require additional specialized information as circumstances of the registrant change, but the basic disclosure of a company's business and financial position is common to all forms.

### Registration and Reporting Under the 1934 Act

Registration under the 1934 Act is a two-fold process. Before a security can be traded in the secondary markets, a registration statement must be on file with both the SEC and the exchange on which the security is to be traded. This requirement holds true even if a registration was made under the 1933 Act. Besides the dual registration, annual and other periodic reports are necessary for a current record of all companies whose securities are traded. When securities are traded on over-the-counter markets, a registration with the SEC is required — except for small companies — and the periodic reporting requirements must be met.

Registration requirements under the Securities Exchange Act of 1934 are almost identical to those of the Securities Act of 1933, so a review of that process need not be given. However, when a company registers its securities with an exchange, some added information is given. Included in the registration with the New York Stock Exchange is a ten-year Summary of Operations (as opposed to five years for the SEC) and a Balance Sheet for two years (one year for the SEC). Where the SEC requires three-year certified statements of Stockholders Equity and Changes in Financial Position, the NYSE requires only two years. Registration on the American Stock Exchange requires a five-year Summary of Operations, three-year statements of Stockholders Equity and Changes in Financial Position, and a Balance Sheet for only one year. Regional exchanges vary in registration requirements.

Chapter 3 gives the forms used for registration with the SEC, and these forms are substantially duplicated for registering with the exchanges. Of more particular concern are (1) a review of the reporting documents submitted annually and quarterly to the SEC and (2) a comparison of these reports with the annual and quarterly reports to stockholders. As noted earlier, future information disclosed in reports to shareholders is expected to more closely parallel information in reports filed with the SEC.

**Annual Reports.** The most common SEC annual report form is Form 10-K. This report must be filed within 90 days of the end of a company's fiscal year. Form 10-K is used to update the information a company gives with the registration statement; hence, the format is very similar to that of an S-1. Compare the following list of disclosure items for Form 10-K to the one given for Form S-1.

Part I

1. Business
2. Summary of Operations
3. Properties
4. Parents and Subsidiaries
5. Pending Legal Proceedings
6. Increases and Decreases in Outstanding Securities
7. Approximate Number of Equity Security Holders
8. Executive Officer of the Registrant
9. Indemnification of Directors and Officers
10. Financial Statements and Exhibits

Part II

11. Principal Security Holders and Security Holdings of Management
12. Directors of the Registrant

13. Remuneration of Directors and Officers
14. Options Granted to Management to Purchase Securities
15. Interest of Management in Certain Transactions

Item 1, Business, covers the same broad spectrum of company operations given in the S-1 and comprises the majority of the narrative in the 10-K. The annual report to stockholders does not generally present such a lengthy discussion, but it is designed to summarize for the investor the business of the firm. In the 10-K which Deseret Pharmaceutical submitted for the fiscal year ending August 31, 1974, nine pages of text explained the business of the firm, compared to two pages of text and pictures in the annual report. With the recent changes in requirements for annual reports, explanation of the business will become more detailed, but the description is still not likely to be as detailed as in the 10-K.

In terms of financial statements (Item 10), any differences that exist between the reports filed with the SEC and those sent to shareholders will be in (1) the extent of detail provided, (2) the number of years for which information is presented and (3) certification requirements. A comparison of Exhibit 4-11 (Statement of Consolidated Income from Form 10-K) with Exhibit 4-12 (Statement of Consolidated Income from Annual Report to Shareholders) illustrates these differences. (Notes to the financial statements would reveal similar types of differences, depending on each company's circumstances.)

In order to provide additional information, most companies include a synthesis of financial data covering a number of years. Exhibit 4-13 shows the Comparative Summary Deseret provided its stockholders. The balance sheet information in both reports is exactly the same. The Form 10-K information serves for both in this instance. (See Exhibit 4-14.)

**Quarterly Reports.** In order to keep both investors and experts apprised of interim changes in a company's operations and financial position, quarterly reports are prepared for stockholders and the SEC. The Commission has recently proposed changes to this form that should make the 10-Q more useful to analysts and investors. The financial data required by the proposals parallels more closely the disclosures required in annual reports to the SEC, but they contain only quarterly and year-to-date information as explained in Exhibit 4-1.

Due to the pending changes in Form 10-Q reporting requirements, exhibits of the new format are not presented. In the author's view, the disclosures will generally be similar to the statements contained in the annual reports. Even with the new requirements, the 10-Q will be a short summary of financial operations when compared to the more detailed annual reports.

Generally stockholders do not receive the 10-Q. Instead, interim reports are sent to the stockholders. In comparative form with brief explanations of a company's continuing operations, these reports present a short summary of sales and income. Deseret Pharmaceutical submitted the financial information shown in Exhibit 4-15 in the quarterly report to stockholders after the second quarter of fiscal 1975.

Quarterly reports are submitted following the first three quarters of a company's reporting year. The annual reports then consolidate the year's operations. During the year, however, significant changes may take place in either a firm's policies or its financial position; and such changes are reported in the 10-Q or quarterly report. To ensure adequate disclosure of any such material event, Form 8-K must be submitted to the SEC within ten days after the end of the month in which a significant event transpired. The following partial list is representative of the items to be reported by Form 8-K:

1. A change in control of the registrant.
2. Acquisition or disposition of a majority-owned subsidiary.
3. The filing or termination of material legal proceedings.
4. A material default on senior security.
5. An increase or decrease of more than five percent in any class of outstanding security.
6. A write-down, write-off, or abandonment of assets.
7. Changes in the registrant's certifying accountants.

Any other event of material importance must also be reported.

As with all other SEC forms, the 8-K has no specific format but is a narrative report of sufficient flexibility that permits management to describe any changes that may affect the firm. Financial statements accompany Form 8-K only when the form is submitted pursuant to an acquisition, and then only when the acquired company represents more than 15 percent of the total assets or revenues of the registering company.

*Exhibit 4-4*

## Use of Proceeds

The net proceeds to be realized by Deseret from the sale of the Common Stock offered hereby, estimated at approximately $5,398,000 after the payment of expenses, are intended to be used approximately as follows:

| | |
|---|---|
| For the construction of additional plant, warehouse and office facilities (see "Property")........ | $1,300,000 |
| For the development and sale of new medical and surgical products (see "Business — Development and Sale of New Medical and Surgical Products")...................................................... | $2,100,000 |
| For the acquisition of certain equipment and systems designed to enable the Company to manufacture component parts and perform operations which are currently being manufactured or performed by suppliers (see "Business — Manufacturing Supplies")...................................... | $ 500,000 |
| For the further development of an asthma drug (see "Business — Research and Development"). | $ 250,000 |
| For other uses .................................................. | $1,248,000 |

The $1,248,000 allocated to "other uses" will be available for such other corporate purposes as management may from time to time deem advisable. See "Business" and "Property".

In addition, a portion of the net proceeds available for "other uses" may be used in connection with the acquisition of companies or products which management believes will enhance Deseret's business. Within the past five years Deseret has made several acquistions for the purpose of integrating operations. Deseret is investigating several acquisition possibilities and intends in the future to seek out and investigate other companies in the medical, surgical or pharmaceutical fields. See "Business — Manufacturing Supplies". Any acquisitions may be made for cash (which may include internally generated funds) or securities of Deseret, or both.

That portion of the net proceeds not required for immediate expenditures will be invested in interest-bearing obligations. Funds so invested are likely to have a rate of return significantly lower than the rate of return realized by the Company in its business operations.

## Exhibit 4-5

## Description of Business

Deseret began its operations in 1956 in the State of Utah as a regional distributor of pharmaceutical products manufactured by others. In 1957 Deseret began to develop, manufacture and sell its own line of disposable surgical and medical products, and in 1967 discontinued its distribution of pharmaceutical products. Since the mid 1960's Deseret has concentrated its primary efforts on the development, manufacture and sale of disposable medical devices delivered to hospitals packaged, sterile and ready for use. As products designed to be used only once, these devices reduce the hazards of cross-infection, eliminate cleaning and resterilizations, and free professional personnel for improved patient care.

## Exhibit 4-6

## Description of Common Stock

The authorized capital stock of Deseret consists solely of 6,000,000 shares of Common Stock, $.50 par value. Each such share is entitled to one vote on all matters to be voted on by stockholders. Voting rights are non-cumulative and the stock is nonassessable. Stockholders are entitled to such dividends as may be declared from time to time by the Board of Directors. In the event of any liquidation or dissolution of the Company, the holders of Common Stock are entitled to receive pro rata all assets remaining after satisfaction of liabilities. Holders of Common Stock have no pre-emptive, subscription or conversion rights and Common Stock is not redeemable, although shares may be repurchased when authorized by the Board of Directors in accordance with Utah law. All of the outstanding shares of Common Stock are, and the shares to be sold pursuant to this Prospectus will be, validly issued, fully paid and nonassessable. To the extent that the foregoing statements are summaries of certain provisions of the Articles of Incorporation of the Company, as amended, the bylaws of the Company, or the statutes of the State of Utah, they are qualified in their entirety by reference thereto.

The Common Stock of Deseret is listed on the American Stock Exchange. The co-transfer agents and co-registrars are Walker Bank & Trust Company, Salt Lake City, Utah, and The Chase Manhattan Bank, N.A., New York, New York.

*Exhibit 4-7*

## Deseret Pharmaceutical Company, Inc. and Subsidiaries
### Statement of Consolidated Income

| | Year Ended August 31 | | | | | Nine Months Ended May 31 | |
| --- | --- | --- | --- | --- | --- | --- | --- |
| | 1967 | 1968 | 1969 | 1970 | 1971 | 1971 | 1972 |
| | | | | | | (Unaudited) | |
| **Continuing operations (Note A):** | | | | | | | |
| Net sales | $4,326,557 | $5,145,734 | $5,887,499 | $6,366,568 | $9,729,431 | $6,966,991 | $9,524,294 |
| Other income | 101,735 | 76,327 | 119,304 | 26,646 | 18,143 | 9,506 | 49,376 |
| Total | 4,428,292 | 5,222,061 | 6,006,803 | 6,393,214 | 9,747,574 | 6,976,497 | 9,573,670 |
| **Costs and expenses:** | | | | | | | |
| Cost of goods sold | 2,412,838 | 2,916,380 | 3,052,710 | 3,880,244 | 4,599,523 | 3,250,083 | 4,173,815 |
| Selling, general, and administrative (Note C) | 584,800 | 719,583 | 1,673,410 | 1,973,405 | 3,004,021 | 2,292,285 | 2,945,463 |
| Interest | | | 13,851 | 112,238 | 49,608 | 48,933 | 2,807 |
| Total | 2,997,638 | 3,636,233 | 4,739,971 | 5,965,887 | 7,653,152 | 5,591,301 | 7,122,085 |
| Income from continuing operations before income taxes and extraordinary item | 1,430,654 | 1,585,828 | 1,266,832 | 427,327 | 2,094,422 | 1,385,196 | 2,451,585 |
| **Federal and state income taxes (Note E):** | | | | | | | |
| Federal — currently payable | 613,025 | 763,255 | 414,480 | 161,828 | 1,061,485 | 649,000 | 1,206,764 |
| Federal — deferred (credit) | 22,200 | 36,400 | 232,700 | 16,884 | (30,249) | 45,000 | (92,217) |
| State | 39,033 | 49,435 | 40,714 | 31,029 | 23,316 | 8,368 | 83,123 |
| Total | 674,258 | 849,090 | 687,894 | 209,741 | 1,054,552 | 702,368 | 1,197,670 |

|  | Year Ended August 31 | | | | | Nine Months Ended May 31 | |
|  | 1967 | 1968 | 1969 | 1970 | 1971 | 1971 | 1972 |
|---|---|---|---|---|---|---|---|
|  |  |  |  |  |  | (Unaudited) | |
| Income from continuing operations before extraordinary item | 756,396 | 736,738 | 578,938 | 217,586 | 1,039,870 | 682,828 | 1,253,915 |
| Extraordinary item — gain on sale of patent and related agreements and equipment, net of applicable income taxes of $48,867 |  |  |  | 126,958 |  |  |  |
| Income from continuing operations, including extraordinary item | 756,396 | 736,738 | 578,938 | 344,544 | 1,039,870 | 682,828 | 1,253,915 |
| Income from operations to be disposed of (Note B) | 250,225 | 178,738 | 274,808 | 222,006 | 144,588 | 114,235 | 271,066 |
| Net income | $1,006,621 | $ 915,476 | $ 853,746 | $ 566,550 | $1,184,458 | $ 797,063 | $1,524,981 |
| Income per share of common stock (Note D): |  |  |  |  |  |  |  |
| Continuing operations before extraordinary item | $ .31 | $ .30 | $ .23 | $ .08 | $ .41 | $ .27 | $ .47 |
| Extraordinary item |  |  |  | .05 |  |  |  |
| Continuing operations, including extraordinary item | .31 | .30 | .23 | .13 | .41 | .27 | .47 |
| Operations to be disposed of | .10 | .07 | .11 | .09 | .06 | .04 | .10 |
| Net income | $ .41 | $ .37 | $ .34 | $ .22 | $ .47 | $ .31 | $ .57 |
| Average number of shares outstanding (Note D) | 2,443,282 | 2,481,066 | 2,499,628 | 2,530,408 | 2,546,858 | 2,545,194 | 2,672,032 |

*Exhibit 4-8*

---

**Deseret Pharmaceutical Company, Inc. and Subsidiaries**
**Consolidated Balance Sheet, May 31, 1972**

### ASSETS
CURRENT ASSETS:

| | | |
|---|---:|---:|
| Cash........................................................ | $ 136,986 | |
| Temporary cash investments (at cost, which approximates market) ............... | 1,883,236 | |
| Accounts receivable: | | |
| Trade (less allowance for doubtful accounts, $99,730)........................ | 2,076,844 | |
| Other (including $63,973 due from officers)........................................ | 97,984 | |
| Inventories (Note 3) ............................. | 2,291,254 | |
| Prepaid expenses and deposits............... | 173,142 | |
| Total current assets ..................... | | $ 6,659,446 |
| INVESTMENT IN SUBSIDIARY TO BE DISPOSED OF (Note 2)........................ | | 2,830,658 |
| PROPERTY — AT COST (Note 4): | | |
| Land ...................................................... | 87,039 | |
| Buildings .............................................. | 718,604 | |
| Machinery and equipment ...................... | 1,277,710 | |
| Construction in progress......................... | 69,887 | |
| Total ............................................... | 2,153,240 | |
| Less accumulated depreciation and amortization...................................... | 510,348 | |
| Property — net........................... | | 1,642,892 |
| DEFERRED COSTS AND OTHER ASSETS: | | |
| Deferred product research and development costs (less accumulated amortization, $630,910) (Note 5)......... | 660,993 | |
| Patents, trademarks, etc. (less accumulated amortization, $57,594).... | 69,935 | |
| Cash surrender value of officers' life insurance — net of related loans of $11,700......................................... | 83,752 | |
| Miscellaneous ....................................... | 40,003 | |
| Total deferred costs and other assets..................................... | | 854,683 |
| TOTAL..................................... | | $11,987,679 |

See Notes to Financial Statements

*Exhibit 4-8*
*(con.)*

---

**Deseret Pharmaceutical Company, Inc. and Subsidiaries**
**Consolidated Balance Sheet, May 31, 1972**

LIABILITIES

CURRENT LIABILITIES:

| | | |
|---|---:|---:|
| Accounts payable — trade..................... | $ 490,124 | |
| Accrued liabilities: | | |
| Income taxes.................................... | 498,308 | |
| Payroll, property, and other taxes........ | 61,548 | |
| Salaries, wages, and commissions ....... | 101,064 | |
| Royalties........................................ | 12,446 | |
| Other.............................................. | 58,904 | |
| Total current liabilities ................. | | $ 1,222,394 |
| DEFERRED INCOME TAXES (Note 6) ......... | | 276,133 |
| COMMITMENTS AND CONTINGENT LIABILITIES (Note 7) | | |
| STOCKHOLDERS' EQUITY (Notes 2 and 9): | | |
| Common stock — $.50 par value per share, authorized, 6,000,000 shares; issued and outstanding, 2,569,192 shares ............................................ | 1,284,596 | |
| Paid-in surplus ..................................... | 3,516,326 | |
| Retained earnings................................. | 5,688,230 | |
| Total stockholders' equity............ | | 10,489,152 |
| | | |
| TOTAL...................................... | | $11,987,679 |

See Notes to Financial Statements.

*Exhibit 4-9*

## Deseret Pharmaceutical Company, Inc. and Subsidiaries

### Statement of Consolidated Stockholders' Equity
### for the Three Years and Nine Months Ended May 31, 1972

| | Common Stock | | Paid-in Surplus | Retained Earnings |
|---|---|---|---|---|
| | Shares | Par Value | | |
| BALANCE, SEPTEMBER 1, 1968 .......................... | 1,194,965 | $1,194,965 | $ 970,800 | $3,234,508 |
| ADD: | | | | |
| Net income ................... | | | | 853,746 |
| Common stock sold under stock option plans | 21,673 | 21,673 | 401,505 | |
| Common stock issued to employees under stock bonus plan................. | 695 | 695 | 36,227 | |
| Reduction in Federal income taxes relating to common stock sold by optionees................... | | | 56,244 | |
| DEDUCT: | | | | |
| Common stock purchased and retired ................ | (2,747) | (2,747) | (30,355) | (29,721) |
| Excess of par value of common stock over the stated value of capital stock of Chemplast, Inc. acquired in a pooling of interest transaction (Note 1) ..... | | | (55,200) | |
| BALANCE, AUGUST 31, 1969 ........................... | 1,214,586 | 1,214,586 | 1,379,221 | 4,058,533 |
| ADD: | | | | |
| Net income ................... | | | | 566,550 |
| Common stock sold under stock option plans | 4,815 | 4,815 | 193,292 | |
| Market value of common stock issued to purchase Chemplast-West, Inc. (Note 1)....... | 3,250 | 3,250 | 50,781 | |
| Reduction in Federal income taxes relating to the exercise of common stock options ............. | | | 61,591 | |
| Other........................... | | | 10,125 | |

*Exhibit 4-9*
*(con.)*

| | | | | |
|---|---|---|---|---|
| DEDUCT — Excess of par value of additional shares of common stock over the stated value of capital stock of acquired subsidiary (Note 1).......... | | | (51,334) | |
| BALANCE, AUGUST 31, 1970............................. | 1,222,651 | 1,222,651 | 1,643,676 | 4,625,083 |
| ADD: | | | | |
| Net income.................... | | | | 1,184,458 |
| Common stock sold under stock option plans | 1,250 | 1,250 | 18,635 | |
| Market value of additional common stock issued to purchase subsidiary (Note 1)...................... | 750 | 750 | 14,625 | |
| Other............................ | | | 17,359 | |
| BALANCE, AUGUST 31, 1971............................. | 1,224,651 | 1,224,651 | 1,694,295 | 5,809,541 |
| ADD: | | | | |
| Net income.................... | | | | 1,524,981 |
| Common stock sold under stock option plans, less related expenses of $23,470..................... | 11,205 | 11,205 | 198,130 | |
| 4% stock dividend — recorded at market value, including cash paid in lieu of fractional shares........................ | 48,740 | 48,740 | 1,571,865 | (1,646,292) |
| Common stock issued in connection with a 2 for 1 stock split in July 1972 (Note 9).............. | 1,284,596 | | | |
| Reduction in Federal income taxes relating to the exercise of common stock options.............. | | | 52,036 | |
| BALANCE, MAY 31, 1972... | 2,569,192 | $1,284,596 | $3,516,326 | $5,688,230 |

See Notes to Financial Statements.

*Exhibit 4-10*

## Deseret Pharmaceutical Company, Inc. and Subsidiaries
## Statement of Consolidated Changes in Financial Position

| | Year Ended August 31 | | | Nine Months Ended May 31,1972 |
|---|---|---|---|---|
| | 1969 | 1970 | 1971 | |
| WORKING CAPITAL PROVIDED: | | | | |
| Continuing operations: | | | | |
| Income from continuing operations before extraordinary item........ | $ 578,938 | $ 217,586 | $1,039,870 | $1,253,915 |
| Expenses not requiring funds in the current period: | | | | |
| Amortization and write-off of deferred product research and market development costs. | 156,679 | 322,077 | 253,512 | 217,782 |
| Depreciation and amortization.......... | 144,930 | 184,378 | 222,950 | 170,733 |
| Deferred income taxes (credit)......... | 232,700 | 16,884 | (30,249) | (20,769) |
| Total funds from continuing operations before extraordinary item.. | 1,113,247 | 740,925 | 1,486,083 | 1,621,661 |
| Extraordinary item, net of applicable income taxes | | 126,958 | | |
| Common stock sold under stock option plans | 321,876 | 198,107 | 19,885 | 209,335 |
| Reduction in Federal income taxes relating to the exercise of common stock options ............. | 56,244 | 61,591 | | 52,036 |
| Market value of common stock issued to purchase Chemplast-West, Inc. ........................... | | 54,031 | 14,625 | |
| Other — net.................. | 33,120 | 18,978 | 51,333 | 23,611 |
| Operations to be disposed of............................. | 182,486 | 303,549 | 160,706 | 245,796 |
| Total working capital provided........ | 1,706,973 | 1,504,139 | 1,732,632 | 2,152,439 |
| WORKING CAPITAL APPLIED: | | | | |
| Purchases of property..... | 221,879 | 323,584 | 238,810 | 342,661 |

Exhibit 4-10
(con.)

| | | | | |
|---|---|---|---|---|
| Additions to deferred charges for product research and market development.................. | 595,741 | 233,609 | 152,268 | 72,274 |
| Reduction in long-term debt.......................... | 250,000 | | | |
| Reclassification of officers' loans receivable. | | 70,040 | | |
| Purchase of subsidiary.... | | 54,031 | 14,625 | |
| Inventories to be sold after one year.............. | | 118,572 | | |
| Cash paid in lieu of fractional shares for stock dividend ..................... | | | | 25,687 |
| Other............................ | 9,957 | 85,416 | 65,219 | 22,423 |
| Operations to be disposed of.............................. | 182,486 | 303,549 | 160,706 | 245,796 |
| Total working capital applied ......... | 1,260,063 | 1,188,801 | 631,628 | 708,841 |
| NET INCREASE IN WORKING CAPITAL......... | $ 446,910 | $ 315,338 | $1,101,004 | $1,443,598 |
| **INCREASE (DECREASE) IN WORKING CAPITAL:** | | | | |
| Current assets: | | | | |
| Cash and temporary cash investments — | $ (131,800) | $ 423,350 | $ 256,121 | $1,278,324 |
| Accounts receivable..... | 130,089 | 438,795 | 249,175 | 174,994 |
| Inventories.................. | 1,182,195 | (113,439) | 208,817 | (7,057) |
| Overpayment of Federal income taxes............ | | 144,186 | | |
| Prepaid expenses and deposits................... | 24,627 | 10,766 | (8,363) | 42,930 |
| Total ................... | 1,205,111 | 903,658 | 705,750 | 1,489,191 |
| Current liabilities: | | | | |
| Notes payable to bank . | (900,000) | (350,000) | 1,250,000 | |
| Accounts payable — trade...................... | (140,933) | (69,537) | 116,167 | (324,421) |
| Income and other taxes | 339,625 | (211,043) | (943,862) | 319,559 |
| Other accrued liabilities | (199) | 23,739 | (26,159) | (62,589) |
| Other......................... | (56,694) | 18,521 | (892) | 21,858 |
| Total ................... | (758,201) | (588,320) | 395,254 | (45,593) |
| NET INCREASE IN WORKING CAPITAL......... | $ 446,910 | $ 315,338 | $1,101,004 | $1,443,598 |

See Notes to Financial Statements.

*Exhibit 4-11*

## Statement of Consolidated Income from Form 10-K
## Deseret Pharmaceutical Company, Inc. and Subsidiaries

The following statement of consolidated income presents, under the caption "continuing operations," the results of operations of the Company and consolidated subsidiaries and, under the caption "income from operations disposed of (Note C)", the net income of Chemplast, Inc. and subsidiaries (disposed of on June 30, 1972). The statement for the four years ended August 31, 1973 has been restated for the change in the method of accounting for product research and development costs as described in Note F to the statements of consolidated income and stockholders' equity.

The statements of consolidated income and stockholders' equity for the three years ended August 31, 1974 have been examined by Haskins & Sells, independent certified public accountants, whose opinion appears elsewhere in this annual report (Form 10-K). These statements should be read in conjunction with their notes and the other consolidated financial statements and their notes included elsewhere herein.

### Statement of Consolidated Income

| | Not Covered by Accountants' Opinion. | | Year Ended August 31 | | |
| --- | --- | --- | --- | --- | --- |
| | 1970 | 1971 | 1972 | 1973 | 1974 |
| Continuing operations: | | | | | |
| Net sales | $6,366,568 | $9,729,431 | $13,460,539 | $18,781,106 | $21,218,919 |
| Interest, dividends, and other income | 26,646 | 18,143 | 77,450 | 479,546 | 560,377 |
| Total | 6,393,214 | 9,747,574 | 13,537,989 | 19,260,652 | 21,779,296 |
| Cost and expenses: | | | | | |
| Costs of products sold | 3,880,244 | 4,599,523 | 6,004,886 | 8,735,106 | 12,193,848 |
| Selling, general, and administrative (Note A) | 1,742,554 | 2,818,114 | 3,512,446 | 4,233,768 | 5,339,330 |
| Product recall and resterilization (Note 5) | | | | | 788,503 |
| Interest | 112,238 | 49,608 | 4,988 | 136,839 | 210,152 |
| Product research and development | 283,000 | 166,695 | 141,790 | | 156,152 |
| Total | 6,018,036 | 7,633,940 | 9,664,110 | 13,105,713 | 18,687,985 |
| Income from continuing operations before income taxes and extraordinary item | 375,178 | 2,113,634 | 3,873,879 | 6,154,939 | 3,091,311 |

| | | | | |
|---|---:|---:|---:|---:|---:|
| Income tax expense (Notes B and 7): | | | | | |
| Federal — currently payable | 161,829 | 1,061,485 | 1,792,376 | 2,680,803 | 1,018,620 |
| State — currently payable | 31,029 | 23,316 | 140,451 | 215,407 | (74,802) |
| Deferred (credit) | (9,191) | (20,643) | 1,000 | 787 | 121,660 |
| Total | 183,667 | 1,064,158 | 1,933,827 | 2,896,997 | 1,065,478 |
| Income from continuing operations before extraordinary item | 191,511 | 1,049,476 | 1,940,052 | 3,257,942 | 2,025,833 |
| Extraordinary item — gain on sale of patent and related agreements and equipment, net of applicable income taxes of $48,687 | 126,958 | | | | |
| Income from continuing operations, including extraordinary item | 318,469 | 1,049,476 | 1,940,052 | 3,257,942 | 2,025,833 |
| Income from operations disposed of (Note C) | 222,066 | 144,588 | 316,060 | | |
| Net income | $ 540,475 | $1,194,064 | $ 2,256,112 | $ 3,257,942 | $ 2,025,833 |
| Income per share of common stock (Notes D and F): | | | | | |
| Primary: | | | | | |
| Continuing operations before extraordinary item | $.07 | $.40 | $.72 | $1.11 | $.69 |
| Extraordinary item | .05 | | | | |
| Continuing operations, including extraordinary item | .12 | .40 | .72 | 1.11 | .69 |
| Operations disposed of | .09 | .06 | .12 | | |
| Net income | $.21 | $.46 | $.84 | $1.11 | $.69 |
| Fully diluted: | | | | | |
| Continuing operations before extraordinary item | $.07 | $.40 | $.71 | $1.10 | $.69 |
| Extraordinary item | .05 | | | | |
| Continuing operations, including extraordinary item | .12 | .40 | .71 | 1.10 | .69 |
| Operations disposed of | .09 | .06 | .12 | | |
| Net income | $.21 | $.46 | $.83 | $1.10 | $.69 |
| The number of shares used in computing per share amounts is as follows: | | | | | |
| Primary | 2,530,408 | 2,546,858 | 2,677,272 | 2,940,940 | 2,920,965 |
| Fully diluted | 2,530,408 | 2,546,858 | 2,712,010 | 2,965,525 | 2,922,650 |

*Exhibit 4-12*

## Statement of Consolidated Income from Annual Report to Shareholders

Statement of Consolidated Income
for the Years Ended August 31, 1974 and 1973

|  | 1974 | 1973 (Note 2) |
|---|---|---|
| NET SALES................................................ | $21,218,919 | $18,781,106 |
| INTEREST, DIVIDENDS AND OTHER INCOME .............................................. | 560,377 | 479,546 |
| Total ............................................... | 21,779,296 | 19,260,652 |
| COSTS AND EXPENSES: |  |  |
| Cost of products sold ............................ | 12,193,848 | 8,735,106 |
| Selling, general and administrative ......... | 5,339,330 | 4,233,768 |
| Product recall and resterilization (Note 4) | 788,503 |  |
| Interest .............................................. | 210,152 |  |
| Product research and development......... | 156,152 | 136,839 |
| Total ............................................... | 18,687,985 | 13,105,713 |
| INCOME BEFORE INCOME TAXES............. | 3,091,311 | 6,154,939 |
| INCOME TAX EXPENSE (Notes 1 and 6): |  |  |
| Current................................................ | 943,818 | 2,896,210 |
| Deferred .............................................. | 121,660 | 787 |
| Total ............................................... | 1,065,478 | 2,896,997 |
| NET INCOME ......................................... | $ 2,025,833 | $ 3,257,942 |
| NET INCOME PER SHARE OF COMMON STOCK (Note 11): |  |  |
| Primary................................................ | $.69 | $1.11 |
| Fully diluted......................................... | $.69 | $1.10 |
| CASH DIVIDENDS DECLARED PER SHARE OF COMMON STOCK............................. | $.44 | None |

## Seven-Year Financial Comparison

## Comparative Summary

Years Ended August 31

| | 1974 | 1973 | 1972 | 1971 | 1970 | 1969 | 1968 |
|---|---|---|---|---|---|---|---|
| Net sales | $21,218,919 | $18,781,106 | $13,460,539 | $9,729,431 | $6,366,568 | $5,887,499 | $5,145,734 |
| Growth rate | 13.0% | 39.5% | 38.3% | 52.8% | 8.1% | 14.4% | 18.9% |
| Cost of goods sold related to sales | 57.5% | 46.5% | 44.6% | 47.3% | 60.9% | 51.8% | 56.7% |
| Selling, general and administrative expenses related to sales | 25.2% | 22.5% | 26.1% | 28.9% | 27.4% | 26.8% | 13.2% |
| Research and development expense | $ 156,152 | $ 136,839 | $ 141,790 | $ 166,695 | $ 283,000 | $ 355,000 | $ 359,335 |
| Income from interest and dividends | $ 560,377 | $ 479,546 | $ 77,450 | | | | |
| Income before income taxes | $ 3,091,311 | $ 6,154,939 | $ 3,873,879 | $ 2,113,634 | $ 375,178 | $ 1,010,204 | $ 1,268,235 |
| Percent of sales | 14.6% | 32.8% | 28.8% | 21.7% | 5.9% | 17.2% | 24.6% |
| Federal and state income taxes | $ 1,065,478 | $ 2,896,997 | $ 1,933,827 | $ 1,064,158 | $ 183,667 | $ 559,580 | $ 690,294 |
| Percent of income before taxes | 34.5% | 47.1% | 49.9% | 50.3% | 49.0% | 55.4% | 54.4% |
| Net income | $ 2,025,833 | $ 3,257,942 | $ 1,940,052 | $ 1,049,476 | $ 191,511 | $ 450,624 | $ 577,941 |
| Percent of sales | 9.5% | 17.3% | 14.4% | 10.8% | 3.0% | 7.7% | 11.2% |
| Return on stockholders' equity | 10.5% | 17.9% | 21.5% | 16.9% | 3.8% | 10.3% | 17.0% |
| Income per share (fully diluted) | $ .69 | $1.10 | $ .72 | $ .41 | $ .08 | $ .18 | $ .23 |
| Net working capital | $11,025,626 | $ 8,951,017 | $ 6,614,400 | $ 3,993,454 | $ 2,663,851 | $ 2,416,352 | $ 2,030,091 |
| Working capital ratio | 2.9 | 5.3 | 5.0 | 4.4 | 2.7 | 3.2 | 8.0 |
| Plant and equipment — net | $ 5,468,006 | $ 2,997,637 | $ 1,726,946 | $ 1,457,507 | $ 1,458,693 | $ 1,239,808 | $ 1,074,922 |
| Total assets — net | $28,226,603 | $20,339,507 | $10,243,193 | $ 9,395,689 | $ 6,061,298 | $ 5,123,402 | $ 3,748,052 |
| Long-term debt | $ 3,000,000 | | | | $ 1,250,000 | $ 900,000 | $ 250,000 |
| Stockholders' equity | $19,291,162 | $18,250,699 | $ 9,042,259 | $ 6,178,501 | $ 5,054,637 | $ 4,379,043 | $ 3,398,646 |
| Per share | $6.60 | $6.15 | $3.33 | $2.43 | $2.00 | $1.75 | $1.37 |
| Average fully dilutive shares outstanding | 2,922,650 | 2,965,525 | 2,712,010 | 2,546,858 | 2,530,408 | 2,499,628 | 2,481,066 |
| Number of employees — year end | 1,728 | 1,064 | 680 | 519 | 550 | 382 | 355 |

Exhibit 4-14

### Deseret Pharmaceutical Company, Inc. and Subsidiaries
### Consolidated Balance Sheet, August 31, 1974 and 1973

| ASSETS | 1974 | 1973 (NOTE 2) |
|---|---|---|
| CURRENT ASSETS: | | |
| Cash (Note 6) .................................... | $   209,081 | $   772,236 |
| Temporary cash investments (at cost, which approximates market) ............... | 100,000 | 2,433,893 |
| Accounts receivable: | | |
| Trade (less allowance for doubtful accounts: 1974, $213, 217; 1973, $171,045)...................................... | 6,164,872 | 4,042,656 |
| Other................................................. | 178,600 | 365,158 |
| Income tax refund receivable ................. | 496,038 | |
| Accrued interest and dividends receivable | 89,140 | 105,829 |
| Inventories (Notes 1 and 3).................... | 9,517,816 | 2,844,114 |
| Deferred income tax charges and other ... | 138,343 | 475,939 |
| Total current assets ........................ | 16,893,890 | 11,039,825 |
| INVESTMENTS IN SECURITIES — At cost (Notes 4 and 6)..................................... | 5,544,190 | 6,109,811 |
| PROPERTY (Note 1): | | |
| Land ................................................... | 163,332 | 163,232 |
| Buildings ............................................. | 2,880,771 | 1,294,897 |
| Machinery and equipment, etc. ............. | 3,150,722 | 2,011,760 |
| Construction in progress........................ | 465,422 | 331,564 |
| Total ............................................... | 6,660,247 | 3,801,453 |
| Less accumulated depreciation .............. | 1,192,241 | 803,816 |
| Property — net............................. | 5,468,006 | 2,997,637 |
| OTHER ASSETS: | | |
| Cash surrender value of officers' life insurance ............................................. | 126,795 | 110,482 |
| Deferred income tax charges.................. | | 12,036 |
| Miscellaneous ...................................... | 193,722 | 69,716 |
| Total other assets ........................ | 320,517 | 192,234 |
| TOTAL..................................... | $28,226,603 | $20,339,507 |

*Exhibit 4-14*
*(con)*

| Deseret Pharmaceutical Company, Inc. and Subsidiaries<br>Consolidated Balance Sheet, August 31, 1974 and 1973 | | |
|---|---|---|
| LIABILITIES | 1974 | 1973<br>(NOTE 2) |
| CURRENT LIABILITIES: | | |
| Note payable to bank (Note 6) | $ 3,000,000 | |
| Accounts payable — trade | 1,676,344 | $ 673,598 |
| Accrued liabilities: | | |
| Salaries, wages and commissions | 514,394 | 302,464 |
| Dividends payable | 177,245 | |
| Income taxes | 107,194 | 864,115 |
| Royalties | 104,813 | 59,684 |
| Payroll, property and other taxes | 83,338 | 79,178 |
| Other | 204,936 | 109,769 |
| Total current liabilities | 5,868,264 | 2,088,808 |
| LONG-TERM NOTES PAYABLE (Note 6) | 3,000,000 | |
| DEFERRED INCOME TAX CREDITS (Note 1) | 67,177 | |
| COMMITMENTS AND CONTINGENT LIABILITIES (Note 8) | | |
| STOCKHOLDERS' EQUITY (Notes 1 and 9): | | |
| Common stock — $.50 par value per share (authorized, 6,000,000 shares; issued: 1974, 2,940,960; 1973, 2,926,884 shares) | 1,470,480 | 1,463,442 |
| Paid-in surplus | 10,589,425 | 10,336,321 |
| Retained earnings (Note 10) | 8,965,729 | 8,185,408 |
| Total | 21,025,634 | 19,985,171 |
| Less 105,040 shares of treasury stock — at cost | 1,734,472 | 1,734,472 |
| Total stockholders' equity | 19,291,162 | 18,250,699 |
| TOTAL | $28,226,603 | $20,339,507 |

*Exhibit 4-15*

*Summary of Financial Operations*
*Form 10-Q*

## CONDENSED FINANCIAL INFORMATION

### OPERATING RESULTS

| | UNAUDITED SECOND QUARTER ENDED FEBRUARY 28, | | UNAUDITED SIX MONTHS ENDED FEBRUARY 28, | |
|---|---|---|---|---|
| | 1975 | 1974 | 1975 | 1974 |
| Net Sales............... | $7,266,000 | $4,498,000 | $12,581,000 | $9,695,000 |
| Net income before federal and state income taxes....... | 1,219,000 | 58,000 | 1,529,000 | 1,531,000 |
| Net income ............ | 670,000 | 143,000 | 896,000 | 928,000 |
| Fully diluted earnings per share...... | $ .23 | $ .05 | $ .31 | $ .31 |
| Fully dilutive shares outstanding......... | 2,964,000 | 2,953,016 | 2,926,742 | 2,973,675 |

### BALANCE SHEET

| ASSETS | FEBRUARY 28, 1975 (UNAUDITED) | AUGUST 31, 1974 (AUDITED) |
|---|---|---|
| Current assets: | | |
| Cash and temporary investments........ | $ 459,000 | $ 309,000 |
| Accounts receivable — trade and other (net)................................... | 6,250,000 | 6,929,000 |
| Inventories.................................... | 11,094,000 | 9,518,000 |
| Other........................................... | 76,000 | 138,000 |
| Total current assets ...................... | 17,879,000 | 16,894,000 |
| Investment in securities*......................... | 5,544,000 | 5,544,000 |
| Property (net).................................... | 6,308,000 | 5,468,000 |
| Other............................................. | 335,000 | 321,000 |
| Total ......................................... | $30,066,000 | $28,227,000 |

Exhibit 4-15
(con.)

Summary of Financial Operations
Form 10-Q

CONDENSED FINANCIAL INFORMATION

BALANCE SHEET

| | FEBRARY 28, 1975 (UNAUDITED) | AUGUST 31, 1974 (AUDITED) |
|---|---|---|
| **LIABILITIES** | | |
| Current liabilities: | | |
| Notes payable to banks...................... | $ 7,500,000 | $ 3,000,000 |
| Accounts payable............................ | 833,000 | 1,676,000 |
| Accrued liabilities ........................... | 1,436,000 | 1,192,000 |
| Total current liabilities ................... | 9,769,00 | 5,868,000 |
| Long-term notes payable ..................... | — | 3,000,000 |
| Deferred income taxcredits................. | 110,000 | 67,000 |
| Stockholders' equity ......................... | 20,187,000 | 19,291,000 |
| Total ...................................... | $30,066,000 | $28,226,000 |

*Market value of these securities was approximately $4,113,000, at March 10, 1975 and $3,670,000 at October 28, 1974.

## SUMMARY

Chapter 3 introduced the reader to the various forms and their uses. Chapter 4, while not analyzing all of the forms, has looked at the most common ones used for SEC registration and reporting and has compared them with annual reports given to stockholders in an actual case setting.

Over the past few years, reporting and disclosure to stockholders has been significantly upgraded. Much of the improvement has come as a result of SEC prompting, but managements have also responded on their own initiative to provide stockholders with more adequate information. The comparisons made in this chapter illustrate some similarities and differences among reports to stockholders and reports to the SEC. Though the detail may seem tedious, the result is that the average American investor has never been more adequately supplied with information concerning companies in which investments are made.

Chapter 5 will focus attention on the interaction between the SEC and the business community, particularly the accounting profession.

## Discussion Questions

1. How many different annual reports do managements prepare? To whom do these reports go?

2. Have there been any significant changes in the disclosure in annual reports to stockholders during the past 40 years? What are they?

3. What are some of the more recent disclosure requirements for annual reports?

4. What are the most common forms sent to the SEC? What information do they contain?

5. What are some of the major differences between the registration reports filed with the SEC and with an exchange?

6. What is the nature of Form 8-K?

7. In what ways will financial statements sent to the SEC be different from financial statements sent to shareholders?

*Chapter 5*   # IMPACT OF THE SEC ON THE ACCOUNTING PROFESSION AND THE BUSINESS COMMUNITY

Two of the most interesting and important current topics concerning the SEC are the role the Commission plays in the development of accounting principles and the impact the SEC has had and will continue to have on the accounting profession and business in general. The variety of responsibilities discussed in earlier chapters pursuant to the SEC's broad statutory powers makes the Commission an important partner in the business community.

In this chapter, the SEC's accounting-related authority is examined. A discussion of accounting practices and problems arising as a result of this legal authority is also presented. Finally, an examination of the interaction of the SEC and the accounting profession in developing accounting principles and auditing standards places this important topic in perspective.

## *SEC AUTHORITY RELATIVE TO ACCOUNTING PRACTICE*

The SEC has the statutory authority to regulate and to prescribe the form, content, and compilation process of financial statements and other reports. This authority has led to a close and continued interaction between the SEC and the accounting profession in the development of financial accounting and reporting principles and practices as well as auditing standards and procedures. A recognition and appreciation of this interaction has been lacking among students of accounting and professionals. It is of interest to examine briefly the reasons why the SEC has been given its broad regulatory authority with respect to financial accounting and reporting practices.

## Congressional Authority

Congress recognized that the SEC would need some control of accounting principles and procedures in order to fulfill its goal of full and fair disclosure. The regulatory authority given to the SEC was considerably influenced by the wide variation in accepted accounting principles and procedures evident in the late 1920s. Some observers felt that this variation may have contributed to the stock market crash and to the decline of the economy in general. In any event, Congress desired to provide adequate disclosure of information for investors and gave the SEC authority to prescribe the accounting principles and procedures to be used in the financial statements it receives.

**Congressional Acts.** The first Congressional grant of accounting authority was to the Federal Trade Commission in the Securities Act of 1933. Section 19(a) of the act delineates this responsibility:

> . . . shall have authority . . . to prescribe the form or forms in which required information shall be set forth, the items or details to be shown in the balance sheet and earning statement, and the methods to be followed in the preparation of accounts, in the appraisal or valuation of assets and liabilities, in the determination of depreciation and depletion, in the differentiation of recurring and nonrecurring income, in the differentiation of investment and operating income, and in the preparation, where the Commission deems it necessary or desirable, of consolidated balance sheets or income statements. . . .

Thus, the 1933 Act gave the FTC, and subsequently the SEC, very broad powers to prescribe any forms, rules, procedures, and regulations it deemed necessary to fulfill its obligations under the law. Included is the authority to have the last word on any accounting matter related to companies filing under the act.

With the 1934 Act and the formation of the SEC, the new Commission inherited the authority of the 1933 Act and received additional authority for companies filing periodic reports. Section 13(b) of the 1934 Act states:

> The Commission may prescribe, in regard to reports made pursuant to this title, the form or forms in which the required information shall be set forth, the items or details to be shown in the balance sheet and the earning statement, and the methods to be followed in the preparation of reports, in the appraisal or valuation of assets and liabilities, . . . etc. (continues in a manner similar to the 1933 Act).

Thus, the regulatory powers relative to accounting practice under the 1934 Act are substantially the same as those under the 1933 Act.

It should be noted that the SEC's authority extends only to companies which must file statements with it. However, due to the interaction between such standard-setting bodies as the American Institute of Certified Public Accountants (and more recently the Financial Accounting Standards Board) and the SEC in developing reporting standards, and due to the size and importance of the filing companies and their auditors, it is probably not an exaggeration to state that the SEC's regulatory power extends, directly or indirectly, to virtually all public accounting situations. Furthermore, because of the provisions in the 1934 Act covering proxy statements, the SEC has been granted regulatory power with respect to the accounting procedures used in preparing the annual reports to the stockholders as well as the reports to the SEC. Under this authority, the new requirements for stockholders' reports were promulgated. (See Chapter 4.)

The Public Utility Holding Company Act of 1935 gives the Commission even broader authority over accounting practice than the 1933 or 1934 Acts. The SEC not only can specify the forms, procedures, and regulations to be used in filing forms with it, but also can specify the accounting system and its function within the registered companies. Section 10(a) contains the following:

> The Commission shall have authority from time to time to make, issue, amend, and rescind such rules and regulations and such orders as it may deem necessary to appropriate. . . . including rules and regulations defining accounting, technical and trade terms used. . . . The Commission shall have authority to prescribe the form . . . in which any statement, declaration, application, report or other document filed with the Commission shall be set forth, the items or details to be shown in balance sheets, profit and loss statements, and surplus accounts, the manner in which the cost of all assets, whenever determinable, shall be shown in regard to such statements, declarations, applications, reports, and other documents filed with the

Commission, or accounts required to be kept by the rules, regulations, or orders of the Commission, and the methods to be followed in
the keeping of accounts and cost accounting procedures and the
preparation of reports, in the segregations and allocation of costs, in
the determination of liabilities . . . depletion and depreciation . . .
income . . . consolidated balance sheets or profit and loss statements
for any companies in the same holding-company system.

The other acts administered by the SEC give added authority in
accounting procedures as they relate to investment companies and
broker-dealers.

**Other Congressional Considerations.** Another factor which
may have led Congress to give the SEC broad power to regulate accounting was the recognized dependence of the investor on the opinion of the accountant. This dependence is noted by Harry A. McDonald, a former Commissioner of the SEC. He said:

> One fact will always be dominant in shaping the course of ac-
> counting — the fact that whether directly or through his advisers,
> whether alone or through the medium of an agency like the SEC, the
> investor cannot help but look to the accountant.[1]

The idea of having government accountants do business auditing
pervaded Congress for a while, but the idea was finally replaced. Instead, Congress recognized the importance of the independent public
accountant and specified that financial statements filed with the SEC
had to be certified by this independent agent.

## *SEC Authoritative Pronouncements*

In exercising the broad regulatory authority described above, the
SEC has primarily relied upon generally accepted accounting principles as established by the accounting profession. However, two important types of documents have been produced by the SEC pursuant to
its legal authority.

Regulation S-X is the principal source relating to the form and
content of financial statements to be included in registration statements and financial reports filed with the Commission, but it does not
contain all of the SEC views on accounting principles. Regulation
S-X, codified in 1940, is continually being revised. Any accountant
involved in SEC registration and reporting must be familiar with S-X

[1]Harry A. McDonald, "How Cooperation in Development of Accounting Principles
by SEC and Profession Helps Investors," *Journal of Accountancy* (March, 1951), p.
415.

and its requirements. Louis H. Rappaport stresses that, "No public accountant should attempt an examination of financial statements intended for filing under any of these Acts without having an up-to-date copy of Regulation S-X at hand."[2]

The other SEC pronouncements of special interest to accountants are the Accounting Series Releases (ASR). These releases primarily explain and clarify accounting procedures and practices needing special treatment, and being of such importance, they require special notice or relation to disciplinary sanctions imposed by the Commission. The releases began in 1937, and as of August, 1975, there were more than 170. Many of these releases, however, have been replaced or modified by subsequent releases.

Just as the Accounting Principles Board (APB) issued authoritative opinions and the Financial Accounting Standards Board (FASB) and the Cost Accounting Standards Board (CASB) now issue standards, the SEC keeps abreast of changing requirements by issuing accounting guidelines as ASRs. A current file is a must for any accountant working with SEC-related reports.

The involvement of the SEC in accounting practice has resulted in a considerable body of literature on accounting principles, and many of the pronouncements carry the force of law, not just recommended adherence. Some examples are discussed below.

## SEC IMPACT
### ON ACCOUNTING AND BUSINESS PRACTICE

There are many areas in accounting and business where the SEC has had a significant influence in the development of current practices. Obviously, not all such areas can be discussed. Specific illustrations presented in this chapter relate to: (1) changes in auditing procedures; (2) increased legal liabilities for managers, accountants, attorneys, and others; and (3) new financial disclosure requirements for businesses.

### Auditing Changes

Though it does not prescribe new auditing standards and procedures, the SEC has had considerable influence over them. By reviewing specific cases, the SEC has highlighted problems and motivated

[2]Louis H. Rappaport, *SEC Accounting Practice and Procedure* (3d ed., New York: Ronald Press, Co., 1972), p. 16.1–16.2.

the accounting profession to take the necessary steps to correct deficiencies by developing additional auditing standards and procedures. The following cases are illustrative.

**The McKesson-Robbins Case.** The *McKesson-Robbins* case shows how an initial SEC review led to subsequent action by the accounting profession and resulted in revised and updated auditing standards.[3] In this well-known case, several millions of dollars of fictitious receivables and inventories were certified by the auditors. The SEC found that the auditing procedures followed were not sufficient, even though they were in accord with the generally accepted auditing procedures at that time. The accounting profession took immediate action in establishing additional standards — the audit practices for confirmation of receivables and for observation of inventories. In view of the responsive action by the accounting profession, the SEC apparently decided to continue to allow the profession to develop auditing procedures, subject to its approval as specified in ASR No. 73.

**The Yale-Express Case.** Another example of SEC action leading to subsequent revision of auditing standards by the accounting profession is the now well-publicized *Yale Express* case.[4] In this case the SEC filed an *amicus curiae* brief stating that accountants have a duty to disclose subsequent discovery of material error existing at the report date in financial statements which were previously certified. This action led to the issuance of a Statement on Auditing Procedure (SAP No. 47) which detailed the procedures to be followed by an auditor upon subsequent discovery of events affecting his opinion upon financial statements previously certified.

**Independence of Accountants.** Another important area in which the SEC has helped develop standards, although in a different manner, is in defining the concept of independence. Although the accounting profession had long realized and required that an auditor must be independent, the SEC, through Regulation S-X, ASR No. 13 (which defines the form of the auditor's certificate), and ASR No. 22 (which defines independence), took the lead in insisting upon the observance of strict rules in determining independence. The accounting profession subsequently incorporated most of the SEC requirements into its code of professional ethics.

[3]*Dennis* v. *McKesson and Robbins, Inc.*, U.S.D.C. District of Columbia Civil Action No. 66 (1938).
[4]*Fisher* v. *Kletz*, 266 F. Supp. 181 S.D.N.Y. (1967).

✓ **Auditing Procedures.** The influence of the SEC on official auditing statements is also apparent. Many of the AICPA's Statements on Auditing Procedure had their beginning as a result of particular cases heard before the SEC. This is not to say that the AICPA Committee on Auditing Procedure has not made an effective contribution. It may, however, suggest the difficulty in determining audit procedures for situations which have not yet occurred and in combating defalcations or other deceptive practices which have not yet happened.

✓ **Fraud Detection.** A final illustration relative to SEC influence on auditing deals with the detection of fraud. Due to its limited number of personnel, the SEC has had to rely on professionals such as accountants, lawyers, and underwriters to assist in the discovery of misrepresentation or fraud. The independent public accountant, because of the thorough examination performed in the audit, is viewed as being in a strategic position to detect any defalcations that could substantially misrepresent the financial position of a firm. As distasteful as this situation is to most practitioners, the SEC seems to be using accountants to assist in its policing efforts.

The impetus for fraud detection seems to be the result of increased litigation generally. To prevent unwanted lawsuits, accountants are being forced to devise stricter audit procedures that have a better chance of detecting fraud at a client company. If accountants are required to concentrate more on fraud detection, future audits will have to be much more extensive and costly. Auditing will become even more elaborate, and managements must be prepared to foot the bill for the expanded review. Naturally, there is opposition to this movement toward greater fraud detection, as evidenced by the following quote:

> The SEC's ideas are directly contrary to a bedrock auditing tenet — that a routine audit can't be relied on to turn up fraud, because such an audit is too limited and the auditor too dependent on figures provided by the client.
>
> A routine audit is designed mainly to make sure that all transactions reported by the company are treated in accord with good accounting practice. . . . Generally accepted auditing standards hold an auditor responsible for failing to uncover fraud only if his failure results from failing to follow generally accepted auditing standards.[5]

[5]Frederick Andrews, "SEC Jolting Auditors Into a Broader Role in Fraud Detection," *Wall Street Journal*, July 12, 1974, p. 1.

However, several large corporate frauds have come to light recently (e.g., the *Equity Funding* case), some of which have been perpetrated for several years. Accountants are having difficulty arguing that a massive swindle is beyond the scope of an audit conforming to generally accepted auditing standards.

Detailed rules for the detection of fraud have not been developed by the SEC. Instead, the Commission has taken a case-by-case approach to enforcement. Without definitive guidelines, the SEC seems to be indicating its expectation that the accounting profession should develop appropriate auditing standards with respect to fraud detection. The final resolution of the accountant's auditing role, especially in connection with fraud detection, is perhaps years away. Auditors must be aware, however, of the changing expectations and requirements so that proper adjustments may be made in the scope of the audit examination.

### Legal Liability

The second area of discussion is that of professional legal liability. An accountant or other professional must be aware of the possibilities of legal action stemming from professional activities. In many cases, knowledge of possible legal consequences of certain actions may make the difference between a successful professional career or a lawsuit which would result in financial ruin and loss of professional reputation.

The increase in litigation during the past few years may be attributed to several causes. First, managements and all professionals have been increasingly subjected to damage suits stemming from their alleged negligence in fulfilling responsibilities. Secondly, banks, other creditors, and investors have found in a number of cases that they have been able to recoup their losses from the managers or from the accountants who prepared and certified the financial statements of the entity. Lastly, there has been a general trend during the past few years towards increasing legal action attempting to hold companies and those associated with them, including accountants, liable to the consuming public.

**Nature of Liability.** To understand the implications of the accountant's legal liability under the Securities Acts, an examination of liability under the common law is necessary. The former liability, an extension of common law liability, is a Congressional attempt to hold accountants and others involved in Securities Acts registrations more strictly liable to third parties than they would be under the common law. Recent cases have expanded the scope of liability under both the common law and the Securities Acts. Thus, an accountant's liability under the common law may be conveniently divided into two parts: (1) liability to clients, and (2) liability to third parties.

*Liability to Clients.* An accountant is liable to clients for negligence in the performance of professional duties and for breach of confidence. Negligence, and not an error in judgement, must be proven and must have resulted in a loss for the client. The accountant must possess the skills reasonably expected of a professional, and must exercise due care in the professional engagement in order to avoid a charge of negligence by a client.[6]

Accountants, like other professionals, acquire a considerable amount of information about their clients. Such information may be harmful to the client if disclosed to the public and competitors, so the law recognizes that the accountant has a fiduciary duty not to disclose confidential information. Since the accountant is considered to have a duty to the public, the recent rise in consumerism has imposed tighter limits on what is considered confidential information between the accountant and the client.

*Liability to Third Parties.* As the fiduciary duty to clients has been limited, liability to third parties and the public has been expanded. Originally, third parties were held to have very limited recovery rights due to the lack of a contractual relationship between the accountant and the third party. A landmark case in the development of liability to third parties was *Ultramares Corporation* v. *Touche*,[7] in which Judge Cardozo of the Court of Appeals ruled that the accountants owed no duty to third parties to perform their examination without negligence. He said:

> Our holding does not emancipate accountants from the consequences of fraud. It does not relieve them if their audit has been so negligent as to justify a finding that they had no genuine belief in its adequacy, for this again is fraud. It does no more than say that, if less than this is proved, if there has been neither reckless misstatement nor insincere profession of an opinion, but only honest blunder, the ensuing liability for negligence is one that is bounded by the contract,

[6]"Legal Liability of Auditors," *Touche-Ross Tempo* (March, 1966), p. 7.
[7]225 N.Y. 170, 174 N.E. 441 (1931).

and is to be enforced between the parties by whom the contract has been made. We doubt whether the average businessman receiving a certificate without paying for it, and receiving it merely as one among a multitude of possible investors would look for anything more.

Judge Cardozo, therefore, set the precedent that accountants would not be liable for mere negligence but would be liable to third parties for fraud and gross negligence amounting to fraud. In subsequent cases the liability to third parties has been extended. It now seems accountants might be held liable to third parties for fraud, gross negligence amounting to fraud, and for ordinary negligence when the accountant knows that the work is being done primarily for the benefit of specified third parties.

Accountants may even be held liable to third parties for ordinary negligence, regardless of who benefits from the work performed. Such a conclusion was suggested as early as 1959 by Professor R. F. Salmonson. His basic reasoning was that as professionals, accountants will rightly be held strictly liable to all who rely on their statements and representations.[8]

The accountant's defense might be adherence to well-defined professional standards. Problems arise, however, when professional standards are under constant review by various policy-making groups, e.g., the FASB, the AICPA, and the SEC. The auditor must stay abreast of any changes in auditing standards if liability is to be minimized.

**Legal Precedents.** The recent *1136 Tenants' Corporation* case may add a new dimension to the auditor's liability to clients and third parties.[9] The lower courts ruled that auditors performing write-up work may be held liable for certain audit procedures even though they did not contract to do an audit. This attempt to further accountants' legal responsibilities may have pronounced effects on the profession. It would at least suggest that accountants should very carefully stipulate in every engagement the responsibility assumed and what procedures will be followed.

The *Continental Vending* case is also significant for two reasons.[10] First, two accountants were held criminally liable even though they

[8]R. F. Salmonson, "CPA's Negligence, Third Parties and the Future," *Accounting Review*, Vol. 34 (January, 1959), p. 91.

[9]*1136 Tenants' Corporation* v. *Max Rothenberg & Company*, 319 N.Y.S. 2d 1007 (1970).

[10]*U.S.* v. *Simon, et. al.*, 425 F 2d 796 (1969).

apparently did not benefit directly from the misstatements in the financial statements. Secondly, it was established by experts that the accountants followed generally accepted auditing procedures (GAAP). The Court of Appeals ruled, however, that the mere following of GAAP may not be enough to hold an accountant guiltless. The accountant must also be sure that the statements certified are not on the whole misleading to the average prudent investor. Following the profession's standards may not be enough in the future. The accountant's work may be judged according to whether or not lay investors would consider the certified financial statements as providing adequate disclosure.

**Provisions Under the 1933 Act.** Liability under the Securities Acts makes even more explicit the need for accountants and managers to be cautious and thorough in financial presentations and audit examinations. Section 11(a) of the 1933 Act provides:

> ... may ... sue — (1) every person who signed the registration statement; (2) every person who was a director of (or person performing similar functions) or partner in, the issuer ... ; (3) every person who with his consent, is named ... as being or about to become a director ... ; (4) every accountant, engineer, or appraiser, or any person whose profession gives authority to a statement made by him, who has with his consent been named as having prepared or certified any part of the registration statement . . .; (5) every underwriter . . .;

The effect of this act on the accountant's liability has been summarized as follows:

1. Any person acquiring securities described in the Registration Statement may sue the accountant, regardless of the fact that he is not the client of the accountant.
2. His claim may be based upon an alleged false statement or misleading omission in the financial statements, which constitutes his *prima facie* case. The plaintiff does not have the further burden of proving that the accountants were negligent or fraudulent in certifying to the financial statements involved.
3. The plaintiff does not have to prove that he relied upon the statement or that the loss which he suffered was the proximate result of the falsity or misleading character of the financial statement.
4. The accountant has thrust upon him the burden of establishing his freedom from negligence and fraud by proving that he had, after reasonable investigation, reasonable ground to believe and did believe that the financial statements to which he certified were true not only as of the date of the financial statements, but

beyond that, as of the time when the Registration Statement became effective.

5. The accountant has the burden of establishing by way of defense or in reduction of alleged damages, that the loss of the plaintiff resulted in whole or part from causes other than the false statements or the misleading omissions in the financial statements. Under the common law it would have been the plaintiff's affirmative case to prove that the damages which he claims he sustained were proximately caused by the negligence or fraud of the accountant.[11]

Important points to note are (1) the accountant can be liable for ordinary negligence to any person acquiring the securities, and (2) the accountant must prove (as opposed to the common law where the plaintiff has the burden of proof) either that the plaintiff's loss resulted from causes other than the misleading statements or that the accountant had, after reasonable investigation, grounds to believe and did believe that the financial statements were true as of the effective date.

The defense outlined under the 1933 Act is called the due diligence defense. That is, the parties to the registration must show that they exercised care in preparing and reviewing not only their part of the forms but also the entire statement. The most important case in this area is *Escott* v. *Barchris Construction Corporation*[12].

In the *Barchris* case, the accountants were held liable for certifying material errors in the financial statements and for conducting an inadequate review. The S-1 review, which is conducted from the date of the certified financial statements until approximately the effective date of the registration, is intended to uncover any information that may indicate that the certified financial statements contain material errors and to satisfy the accountant's due diligence requirement.

**Stipulations of the 1934 Act.** It was generally believed until a few years ago that the principal liability threat for the business community under the 1934 Act was Section 18. The applicable part reads as follows:

Any person who shall make or cause to be made any statement in any application, report, or document filed pursuant to this title or any rule or regulation thereunder or any undertaking contained in a

[11]Saul Levy, *C.P.A. Handbook* (New York: American Institute of Certified Public Accountants, 1952), p. 39.
[12]283 F. Supp. 643 S.D.N.Y. (1968).

registration statement as provided in subsection (d) of section 15 of this title, which statement was at the time and in the light of the circumstances under which it was made false or misleading with respect to any material fact, shall be liable to any person (not knowing that such statement was false or misleading) who, in reliance upon such statement, shall have purchased or sold a security at a price which was affected by such statement, for damages caused by such reliance, unless the person sued shall prove that he acted in good faith and had no knowledge that such statement was false or misleading. . . .

Under the 1934 Act, the accountant is generally liable only to the date of financial statements, not the effective date as under the 1933 Act. Management, however, assumes liability for the financial statements as long as they are used by the third parties. Also, a plaintiff must prove (as opposed to the 1933 Act where the accountant/manager has burden of proof) that personal reliance upon the financial statements was the actual cause of damages incurred. Finally, the accountant is apparently not liable to third parties for ordinary negligence since it must be shown only that the accountant acted in good faith and had no knowledge that the statements were misleading. Managements assume responsibility for ordinary negligence. This is equivalent to the common law liability to third parties.

In addition to Section 18, liability has recently been found under Section 10(b) of the 1934 Act. In the now famous case involving Yale Express Systems, Inc., a major accounting firm was held liable under Rule 10b-5 which states:

It shall be unlawful for any person, directly or indirectly, by the use of any means . . .
(a) to employ any device, scheme, or artifice to defraud,
(b) to make any untrue statement of a material fact or to omit to state a material fact necessary in order to make the statements made, in the light of the circumstances under which they were made, not misleading, or,
(c) to engage in any act, practice, or course of business which operates or would operate as a fraud or deceit upon any person, in connection with the purchase or sale of any security.

The accounting firm failed to disclose information which it obtained in a management services engagement subsequent to an audit engagement. The information indicated that the financial statements which the firm certified as a result of the audit contained false and misleading statements. The court held that the accounting firm's silence amounted to a device to omit a material fact necessary to make the statements not misleading (Rule 10b-5 above). This decision had a significant influence on auditing procedures, and it led to the issuance of SAPs 41 and 47. Through the use of Rule 10b-5, it may be possible for plaintiffs to circumvent the defenses of the accountant under Section 18. Managements have been held liable under Rule 10b-5 on numerous occasions, and the rule now poses major liability implications for accountants.

**Future Issues.** The issue of professional liability is not settled. Lawrence E. Nerheim, General Counsel of the SEC, stated that the Commission has never filed an *amicus* brief on behalf of an accountant to prescribe some limit to liability. He states, " . . . perhaps, just perhaps, the time has arrived. But the questions remain: (1) where does the liability stop? And (2) for what kind of conduct or misconduct should the accountant be liable in damages?"[13] These important questions must yet be realistically answered.

## Disclosure Requirements

As has been mentioned previously, an essential objective of the SEC is to provide full and fair disclosure of financial and other information for investors. Therefore, it should not be surprising that the SEC has had a significant impact upon the reporting requirements of businesses. Often at the urging or insistence of the SEC, requirements for both the amount of information disclosed and the extent of detail provided are increasing. Support for this statement was presented in the previous chapter, where the additional reporting requirements for the annual report to shareholders were outlined. In effect, the SEC now requires that information similar to that filed with the SEC on Form 10-K be reported to shareholders.

**Segment Reporting of Diversified Companies.** Additional evidence can be seen by considering the historical development of lines-of-business reporting. During the early- and mid-1960s, many companies which were unrelated in terms of product lines were merging. This caused considerable interest in a proposal to require these diversified companies (often called conglomerates) to report their sales and profits by major segments of the company. Manuel Cohen, then chairman of the SEC, took the lead in advocating this type of reporting. Due to pressure from the SEC, members of the financial community

---

[13]Lawrence E. Nerheim, *Journal of Accountancy*, (December, 1974), p. 10.

(including the Financial Executives Institute, the Accounting Principles Board, and the National Association of Accountants) conducted studies concerning the desirability and feasibility of reporting by segments of diversified companies. While the actual recommendations for disclosing segmental information initially came from groups other than the SEC, most notably the FEI, they were prompted by the SEC. In 1969, amendments to Forms S-1, S-7, and 10 were adopted by the SEC. These amendments required disclosure of sales and profit information by lines of business. Later these requirements were extended to the 10-K and, as mentioned earlier, are now incorporated in the annual report to shareholders.

**Lease Reporting.** Another example of the SEC's influence upon reporting requirements deals with leases. The APB issued four opinions (No. 5, No. 7, No. 27, and No. 31) dealing with leases; and the FASB currently has the topic under consideration. Notwithstanding this activity by the accounting profession, in 1973 the SEC issued ASR No. 147 (which requires disclosures that go beyond those already provided in the APB opinions). In effect, the SEC now requires disclosure of the impact on net income as if noncapitalized leases were capitalized. Whether or not such disclosures are appropriate is debatable, but the point is that the influence of the SEC on disclosure requirements is significant and pervasive.

**SEC Disclosure Recommendations.** Sometimes the SEC does not require disclosures as such, but strongly encourages reporting companies and accountants to present certain information. Such is the case with ASR No. 166 which urges companies in their 1974 financial statements to make "substantial and specific disclosure as to significant and increasing business uncertainties." Illustrative of the types of recommended disclosures are situations where there have been substantial changes in marketable securities portfolios, loan portfolios (even where increased provisions for losses have been made), and where a small number of projects may dominate the net effect of operating results. The release states "when unusual circumstances arise or where there are significant changes in the degree of business uncertainty existing in a reporting entity, a registrant has the responsibility of communicating these items in its financial statements."[14]

[14]ASR No. 166.

## Summary of the SEC's Impact on Procedures, Liability, and Requirements

Changes in auditing procedures, extension of legal liability, and additional disclosure requirements are three major areas where the SEC has had an important influence. In auditing, the influence has been mainly to expand the scope of the auditor's examinations and the procedures used in an audit. Fraud detection has only recently been emphasized in an auditor's review. Accountants still argue that fraud detection is not the primary purpose of an audit, but recent emphasis seems, nonetheless, to be forcing this role upon auditors with attendant implications for mangements.

Legal liability is an increasingly important topic for accountants and managers. Under the common law, accountants are liable to their clients for certain breaches of confidential information and for ordinary negligence leading to a client's loss. Liability is also possible to third parties for fraud, gross negligence amounting to fraud, and ordinary negligence, if the accountant's work was primarily for the benefit of third parties. While management is generally liable, third parties must prove that the accountant's work led to their losses before liability can be established. Indications point to the possibility that accountants will be held more strictly liable to third parties for ordinary negligence in the future. The extent of that liability has not yet been determined by the courts; however, it may extend to those third parties claiming a special benefit from the accountant's work or to anyone whose reliance on the independent public accountant's opinion based upon misleading statements resulted in a loss.

Under the 1933 Act, professionals are liable for ordinary negligence to all third parties buying securities registered under registration statements containing certified financial statements with material errors. The liability under Section 18 of the 1934 Act is, in many respects, similar to that under the common law. However, recent decisions have held accountants liable under Rule 10b-5. This rule may in the future enable third parties to circumvent the common law defenses of the accountant and businessperson and to hold them to liability similar to that under the 1933 Act. Future court cases will be needed to resolve this question.

It was long believed that accountants could escape liability in any form by adhering to the standards of the profession as determined by the AICPA, the SEC, and other authoritative bodies. However, the decision in *Continental Vending* in which financial statements were held to be misleading on the whole although no specific accounting procedures were violated may eventually controvert that belief.[15] Independent public accountants could eventually be forced to determine in each case whether financial statements upon which they are offering an opinion (and possibly even those with which they are just associated) will be misleading to the average prudent investor. This will require not only a strict adherence to current professional standards and procedures, but also the development of additional standards and considerable judgment on the part of the accountant.

Disclosure, one of the primary purposes of securities legislation, is intended to provide investors with sufficient information to make informed investment decisions. The SEC has been consistently urging improved disclosure in all reports prepared by corporations. Recent changes in reporting requirements highlight the lengthy effort of the Commission to have corporate information available to the consuming public.

# DEVELOPMENT OF
## ACCOUNTING PRINCIPLES

The Commission's official philosophy has been, from the beginning, to allow the accounting profession to develop generally accepted accounting principles. In 1938, ASR No. 4 stated:

> In cases where financial statements filed with this Commission pursuant to its rules and regulations under the Securities Act of 1933 or the Securities Exchange Act of 1934 are prepared in accordance with accounting principles for which there is no substantial authoritative support, such financial statements will be presumed to be misleading or inaccurate despite disclosures contained in the certificate of the accountant or in footnotes to the statements provided the matters involved are material. In cases where there is a difference of opinion between the Commission and the registrant as to the proper principles of accounting to be followed, disclosure will be accepted in lieu of correction of the financial statements themselves only if the points involved are such that there is substantial authoritative support for the practices followed by the registrant and the position of the Commission has not previously been expressed in rules, regulations or

[15]*U.S.* v. *Simon, et. al.*, 425 F 2d 796 (1969).

other official releases of the Commission, including the published opinions of its Chief Accountant.

This release is important and deserves analysis. The Commission requirement is two-fold. First, in order to be accepted by the SEC at all, financial statements must be prepared in accordance with accounting principles which have "substantial authoritative support." If the accounting principles used do not have substantial authoritative support, they are presumed *prima facie* false or inaccurate despite any disclosures. Secondly, if the Commission disagrees with the registrant and the accounting principles used have substantial authoritative support, the SEC will accept footnotes to the statements in lieu of correcting the statements to the SEC view only if the SEC has not previously expressed its opinion on the matter in published material.

Two points here are critical to an understanding of the relationship of the SEC and accounting principles. First, the SEC reserved the right explicitly (which it would have anyway under its general powers) to rule against a registrant even if it follows principles having substantial authoritative support. Secondly, the SEC reserved the right to determine what principles have substantial authoritative support.

## Government Involvement in Developing Principles

Traditionally, the Commission has looked to the accounting profession to take the lead in developing principles that would have official support. The APB was established by the AICPA to formulate such authoritative principles. In 1973, the FASB replaced the APB as the official policymaking body. The FASB received an official vote of confidence from the SEC with ASR No. 150. It states:

Various Acts of Congress administered by the Securities and Exchange Commission clearly state the authority of the Commission to prescribe the methods to be followed in the preparation of accounts and the form and content of financial statements . . . and the responsibility to assure the investors are furnished with information necessary for informed investment decisions. In meeting this statutory responsibility effectively, in recognition of the expertise, energy and resources of the accounting profession and without abdicating its responsibilities, the Commission has historically looked to the standard setting bodies designated by the profession to provide leadership in establishing and improving accounting principles.

> The body presently designated by the . . . AICPA to establish accounting principles is the Financial Accounting Standards Board (FASB).

> Principles, standards, and policies promulgated by the FASB in its Statements and Interpretations will be considered by the Commission as having substantial authoritative support, and those contrary to such FASB promulgation will be considered to have no such support.

Despite these statements outlining the SEC's desire for the profession to take the lead in developing principles, the Commission has not always expressed unqualified confidence in the profession's ability and performance. Several SEC officials have indicated during the past few years that the profession has not adequately fulfilled its role in developing accounting principles. A statement by Commissioner Woodside is typical of those somewhat critical of the profession. After stating that the Commission has, in general, followed a policy of allowing the profession to develop principles, he states:

> It may also be that we should have made greater use of our Accounting Series Releases to announce firm policies on more accounting matters.

> Certainly, if the academic and operating branches of the accounting profession continue to join certain analysts and commentators in suggesting the absence of accounting principles and the noncomparability, and therefore the limited usefulness, of corporate financial statements, it will become increasingly difficult as a policy matter for us to justify and rely upon Accounting Series Release No. 4 and Rule 2-02 of S-X, which governs the content of a certificate.[16]

A more recent statement from A. A. Sommer, Jr., a SEC Commissioner states:

> Very frankly, I am troubled as I read the history of the last forty years' effort of the accounting profession to establish a system of viable accounting principles. The FASB is the third structure created for the purpose; it is the third effort to avoid in the future the disillusionments with financial reporting that have recurred with dismaying frequency; it is the third chance of the profession to prove that the Commission can safely entrust leadership in this task to the profession. These forty years have been characterized by alternating Commission moods of warm confidence in the ability of the profession to do the job and intense criticisms of the failures of the profession.

[16]Byron D. Woodside, "Address Before Hayden Stone Accounting Forum," *Journal of Accountancy*, (February, 1966), p. 51.

As one reads this history, and then looks at the continuing problem with adequate financial reporting, one is tempted to conclude that indeed the Commission should undertake a full exercise of its statutory powers and through its own efforts, bring forth a sufficient, workable set of accounting principles.[17]

Considering this criticism, it is not surprising that some feel a shift from the private to the public sector is taking place. While the APB published its last six opinions, the SEC issued 14 Accounting Series Releases. During the first year of the FASB, the SEC published 20 ASRs, prompting the chairman of the FASB, Marshall S. Armstrong, to remark that the SEC was doing much more than the private sector. In fact, he continued, ASR No. 147 can be viewed as the SEC preempting the private sector in the establishment of the GAAP.[18]

Another leading expert, Leonard M. Savoie, said:

> For sentimental reasons I still prefer to see accounting standards set in the private sector, but I can no longer advocate this position with great conviction. My reasons are that standards are now being determined largely in the public sector, and inevitably the function will be taken over completely by the public sector. The SEC occupies a dominant position in determining accounting standards and the APB a subordinate one. The FASB will have the identical relationship with the SEC . . . that is, the SEC will be dominant and the FASB will be subordinate.[19]

Others have made the point even stronger. Professor Charles T. Horngren, a member of the APB from 1969 through 1973, stated:

> It is time to dispel the oft-heard myth that a private group is setting the accounting principles which are then enforced by the policing agency, the SEC. The job of devising accounting principles is a joint effort, a private-public institutional arrangement that should be explicitly admitted and publicized forthrightly. . . . Moreover, the constraints affecting both the SEC and the APB should also be recognized.[20]

---

[17]Securities and Exchange Commission, "The SEC and the FASB: Their Roles," news release of January 21, 1974, (Washington: U.S. Government Printing Office, 1974). A. A. Sommer, Jr. delivered this speech at the University of Washington, Seattle, Washington, on January 21, 1974.

[18]Marshall S. Armstrong, reported in *Journal of Accountancy* (March, 1974), pp. 9–10.

[19]Leonard M. Savoie, "Accounting Attitudes . . .," *Financial Executive* (October, 1973), pp. 78–80.

[20]Charles T. Horngren, "Accounting Principles: Private or Public Sector?" *Journal of Accountancy* (May, 1972), p. 39.

Even though the SEC possesses legal authority to control accounting procedures and form, most accountants still believe that the development of accounting principles should come almost entirely from within the profession. The plain truth is, however, that the SEC has had a broad influence in the development of generally accepted accounting principles. The SEC has been described as top management and the accounting profession as the frontline management; when top management dislikes a decision that has been made, the decision is altered. The chief accountant for the SEC, John C. Burton, disagreed with this position but commented on the possibility of future SEC involvement:

> . . . we are in partnership . . . we do not want to be senior partner, although it might turn out that way — depending on how the profession moves.[21]

The cause of increasing involvement by the public sector has been clearly stated by Savoie:

> . . . the failure of business and the accounting profession to accept the authority of APB rules and regulations is the main reason its [the SEC] function has moved further into the public sector.[22]

The business community and the accounting profession, by their own hesitance to comply with APB pronouncements, have apparently brought about increased government involvement in the establishment of GAAP. Thus, only if the FASB responds quickly to problems and if corporate managements and accounting practitioners give credence to the statements of the FASB will the trend be altered.

## The Investment Credit: An Example

Perhaps a specific case involving the investment credit will help to illustrate. In the Revenue Act of 1962, Congress created a new taxation concept called the investment credit. The investment credit is a certain percentage of the cost of some depreciable assets used to offset income tax payable in the year the assets are purchased. The APB considered the various accounting treatments possible for the investment credit and issued its Opinion No. 2, setting forth what it believed to be the correct method. Basically, the APB decided that the

[21]"Paper Shuffling and Economic Reality," *Journal of Accountancy* (January, 1973), p. 28.
[22]Savoie, *op. cit.* See also Richard T. Baker, *Financial Executive* (January, 1972), p. 16.

allowable investment credit should be reflected in net income over the productive life of the acquired property and not just in the year in which it was placed in service.

The SEC did not support the APB and it concluded, in ASR No. 97, that two methods would be acceptable; these were (1) essentially the same method proposed by the APB or (2) a method in which a significant percentage of the investment credit would be taken as a reduction of income tax liability in the year of acquisition, the remainder being deferred until future years. This method had been considered and rejected by the APB.

The SEC's position reflected the lack of support by corporate managers and accounting practitioners of the APB action. Many financial statements were subsequently certified even though their treatment of the investment credit was contrary to APB requirements. This happened despite a plea from the AICPA President Robert E. Witschey for AICPA members to qualify their opinions on statements of companies not following the APB position.

In view of the lack of general acceptance of its opinion, in 1964, the APB reconsidered and issued Opinion No. 4 which stated that although it preferred the method outlined in Opinion No. 2, the APB would accept the so-called "full-flow-through" method. This method considered the investment credit to be a reduction of taxes in the year of acquisition only. The SEC then issued revised regulations which were substantially (with some differences of form) the same as those of Opinion No. 4.

The latest round in the investment credit battle portrayed the impotence of both the APB and the SEC when Congress and public opinion went against them. This series of events lends strong credence to the statement by Professor Horngren that "setting accounting principles is indeed subject to popularity testing."[23]

The investment credit was repealed by Congress but was subsequently reinstated in 1971. The APB issued an exposure draft to its members in October, 1971, after receiving a commitment from the SEC in support of its position and from the Treasury Department to remain neutral. The Senate Finance Committee issued its version of the 1971 Revenue Act in November; in response to lobbying by industry groups, the Finance Committee indicated that companies

---

[23]Horngren, *op. cit.*, p. 40.

should be free to choose alternative methods of accounting for the investment credit. Several days later, the Treasury Department sent to the Chairman of the Senate Finance Committee a letter indicating support for a continuation of the optional treatment previously used. Congress then destroyed both the APB and SEC positions by passing legislation that no taxpayer could be required to use any one particular method against personal consent.

The investment credit situation is but one case illustrating how the APB did not have the last word on accounting principles, as many have assumed. Its opinions were subject to SEC, industry, and Congressional support. Doubtlessly, the FASB will have to be prepared to operate in this environment as well.

## SUMMARY

In the author's view, the SEC has significantly influenced the accounting profession and the business community. The SEC's influence is viewed as an important factor in determining generally accepted accounting principles and auditing standards as well as business practices. A continual revitalization of the accounting profession will be necessary if a viable partnership is to be maintained. Commissioner Sommer summarizes the dilemma:

> It seems likely that this tremendous effort (the FASB) we are all about is the last opportunity to keep this job out of the hands of government and, therefore, I think it is important that everyone involved do, in the vernacular, their damndest to make the effort work. This means industry, profession, Commission — for I repeat, another failure will produce irresistible insistence that the chore be removed to other hands.[24]

The challenge to accountants and business executives is real, exciting, and potentially rewarding.

---

[24]Securities and Exchange Commission, *loc. cit.*

## Discussion Questions

1. Why has the SEC been given such broad statutory power in relation to accounting principles and procedures?

2. How was the SEC granted this power? Trace the events.

3. What is Regulation S-X?

4. What are Accounting Series Releases? What is their purpose?

5. Discuss some of the instances in which the SEC has exerted influence upon auditing standards and the significance of these influences.

6. What is the accounting profession's view of fraud detection in an audit? What seems to be the SEC position?

7. What factors have led to the current emphasis upon the legal liability of auditors in connection with publicly issued financial statements?

8. In what main areas are accountants' legal liabilities grouped?

9. Why is the SEC involved in disclosure issues? What are some of the primary areas of interest where the SEC has been an important motivator of additional disclosure?

10. How has the SEC generally elected to fulfill its responsibilities with regard to accounting principles?

11. What seems to be the current trend of the SEC action in regard to accounting principles?

12. Should GAAP be promulgated in the private or public sector?

# APPENDIX
# SELECTED REFERENCES

## *Primary Sources*

1. The acts as amended, and rules and regulations for each of the acts. The rules and regulations are official explanations and interpretations of the acts. Copies of the acts and the rules and regulations may be purchased from the Government Printing Office, Washington, DC 20402.

2. Regulation S-X. This is the basic document that explains the accounting procedure to be used in connection with forms filed with the SEC. The regulation is amended frequently and care should be taken to ensure proper understanding of the amendments. Copies can be purchased from the Government Printing Office.

3. Accounting Series Releases. The SEC uses the ASRs to explain or clarify any desired changes in accounting or auditing procedures in reports filed with the SEC. A complete list should be maintained as a necessary correlative to SEC-related accounting work.

## *Additional Sources*

### 1. Professional Services

A. *Federal Securities Law Reporter* (Chicago: Commerce Clearing House, Inc.) This four-volume reference work contains indexes and cross-references and has interpretations of all of the acts, cases, procedures, and current material.

B. *Securities Regulations* (Englewood Cliffs: Prentice-Hall). This three-volume work has indexes and cross-references and contains summaries of all the acts, cases, and interpretations of procedures and rules. Continual updating is an important feature of this service.

C. Several accounting firms have SEC departments and provide books and manuals for training and informing their staffs. While these materials may be somewhat difficult for the casual student to get, the serious researcher will find the accounting firms cooperative and their material useful. In addition, most large accounting firms provide up-to-date information to their clients. Some examples of these reports are:

   (1) *Accounting Events and Trends*, by Price Waterhouse & Co.
   (2) *Touche-Ross Tempo*, by Touche-Ross & Co.
   (3) *SEC Newsletter*, by Laventhos & Horwath.
   (4) *The Week in Review*, by Haskins & Sells.
   (5) *Executive News Briefs*, by Arthur Andersen & Co.

D. The Practicing Law Institute in New York has sponsored numerous conferences on securities problems. The conferences are reported in equally numerous publications. Check legal libraries for a complete list, but among the most helpful are:

(1) *Annual Institute on Securities Regulation* (Six annual meetings and books as of 1975).

(2). *Disclosure Requirements of Public Companies and Insiders* (1967).

(3) *New Trends and Special Problems Under the Securities Laws* (1970).

(4) *Going Public: Filing Problems* (1970).

(5) *How to Go Public* (1971). Has annual updates.

(6) *The SEC Speaks* (1972).

## 2. Textbooks

There are a number of lengthy, technical texts on the SEC. The following is not a comprehensive list, but it will give the serious student an adequate start for research.

A. Bloomenthal, Harold S. *Securities and Federal Corporate Law*. New York: Clark Boardman Co., 1972. This book provides a technical review of the legal problems involved in securities registration. This is a "how-to-do-it" book of instructions for practitioners. Probably found in legal libraries.

B. Folk, Ernest L. III. *Securities Law Review*. New York: Clark Boardman Co., 1974. Each year an additional volume of this series is published. The format is a book of articles on various subjects of interest in the securities field.

C. Jennings, Richard W., and Harold Marsh, Jr. *Securities Regulations: Cases and Material*. Mineola: Foundation Press, 1972. Designed as a classroom case reference, the book is useful for researching cases and their implications. This book is supplemented annually with current material.

D. Kellogg, Howard L., and Morton Poloway. *Accountant's SEC Practice Manual*. Chicago: Commerce Clearing House, 1971. A practical guide and reference that explains the why's and wherefore's of preparing SEC reports and registrations.

E. Lasser, J. K., and J. A. Gerardi. *Federal Securities Act Procedure*. New York: McGraw-Hill Book Co., 1934. Written at the time the acts were inaugurated, the book provides a contemporary look at the controversy and passage of the securities laws.

F. Loss, Louis. *Securities Regulation*. Boston: Little, Brown & Co., 1961. Professor Loss has not only written the text, but also provides periodic supplements that keep the text current. Explanations of current problems and new procedures are given.

    G. Rappaport, Louis H. *SEC Accounting Practice and Procedure*, 3d ed. New York: Ronald Press Co., 1972. Rappaport's treatise on the SEC has proven helpful for many years. The book is thorough, yet easy to read and understand.

    H. Robinson, Gerald J., and Klaus Eppler. *Going Public*. New York: Clark Boardman Co., 1974. An explanation of the problems of underwriting. Another "how-to" book for practitioners.

    I. Sowards, Hugh L. (ed.). *Business Organizations: The Federal Securities Act*. 2 vols. New York: Matthew Bender & Co., 1973. Another legal approach to understanding securities problems, and it provides an historical background. Again, available in legal libraries. Volume 2 of this series is comprised of seven volumes of technical material.

## 3. SEC Publications

    A. *Annual Reports*. Each fiscal year a summary of SEC activity is given to Congress in an annual report. The reports contain statistical information as well as narrative explanations of procedures and activities. Available from the Government Printing Office or in most university libraries.

    B. *News Digest*. A brief summary of financial proposals to and action by the SEC. Useful for an interim review of SEC registrations and actions taken by the SEC.

    C. *SEC Docket*. A weekly review of the official releases and statements by the SEC. Contains current cases and litigation together with the disposition of the cases.

    D. *The Work of the Securities and Exchange Commission*. This pamphlet is a brief explanation of the history and function of the Commission. The most recent issue is April, 1974.

    E. *Statistical Bulletin*. Contains complete statistics on securities traded, market activity, securities offerings, and registrations. A tool for statistical research in securities markets.

    F. The SEC commissioner and officers often give speeches to various university and professional groups. These speeches are usually published and are available at most SEC offices. The speeches are one way to keep current on SEC thinking and emphasis.

    G. The Commission publishes many additional pamphlets on specific problems and ideas. Most university libraries will have a rather complete set.

## 4. Periodicals

The list of periodicals containing SEC-related material is endless. The following is a selected list of some that should prove useful.

A. *Financial Analysts Journal.* This professional journal has a monthly section on securities laws and problems. In addition to the summary of current problems, frequent articles explain more carefully the various aspects of securities statutes.

B. *Financial Executive.* Another professional journal that has carried numerous articles on various aspects of securities laws. The articles are well-documented and useful for staying abreast of securities problems.

C. *Journal of Accountancy.* A well-known accounting publication, the *Journal* often has articles and comments relative to SEC practice or the interaction of the AICPA and the SEC.

D. *Review of Securities Regulation.* Published by Standard & Poors Corporation, this work analyzes current laws and regulations affecting the securities industry.

E. *Securities Regulation and Law Report.* A weekly publication of the Bureau of National Affairs, Washington, D.C., designed to inform professionals on current topics and problems.

F. *Securities Regulation and Transfer Report.* This short newsletter, published by Management Reports, Inc., Boston, provides a look at current matters and an explanation of effects on management. Generally available at legal libraries.

G. Most law schools have periodic "Law Reviews." These publications often have SEC-related articles that are useful sources of current legal explanations.

H. Business periodicals often carry short articles or comments on the SEC. While the articles are not always scholarly, they do inform readers of current, practical matters. Magazines such as *Business Week, Fortune,* and *Nation's Business,* along with the *Wall Street Journal* and the "Business and Finance" section of each Sunday's *New York Times* are useful for the accountant and businessperson.

I. Several state CPA societies, in addition to the AICPA, publish journals that have articles on the SEC. Check with the professional organization in your state for any additional information that may be available.

J. Many colleges of business publish scholarly journals that provide useful research articles on the SEC. *Harvard Business Review* and *Columbia Journal of World Business* are just two such examples. See the periodicals listing at universities for other journals.

## 5. Other

A. Ainsworth, LeRoy G., and Johnny S. Turner. *An Overview of the SEC with a Guide to Researching Accounting-Related SEC Problems.* Provo: Brigham Young University Press, 1971. A small monograph useful in designing research on the SEC.

B. Brombert, Alan R. *Securities Law: Fraud.* New York: McGraw-Hill Book Co., 1973. This three-volume set provides an historical and current perspective on Rule 10b-5. Recent expansion of fraud detection is discussed and illustrated.

C. Haining, Hazel E. "Federal Regulation of the Securities Industry." Doctoral dissertation, Lincoln, Nebraska, 1972. This provides an examination of the events leading to and some of the results of the federal statutes governing the securities markets.

D. Knauss, Robert L. *Securities Regulation Sourcebook.* New York: Practicing Law Institute, 1972. A single-volume collection of the most important reference materials on securities regulations. The book accomplishes its purpose in a complete but technical way.

# DISCUSSION POINTS

## CHAPTER 1

1. When the economic system was basically a barter economy, the management and owners of a business were usually the same individuals. External reporting of financial data was not necessary. However, as business activity increased in size and complexity, external financing became more common. This growth of businesses led to extensive use of the corporate form of business; thus, ownership and management became separated. This separation necessitated the need for objective verification of data and created a need for disclosure of information to owners and potential investors. However, there were abuses of trust and losses of invested capital and securities. Thus, the government began to step in and require businesses to publicly disclose their activities.

2. No, the first attempt at securities regulation occurred as early as 1902. However, three major bills which were introduced before 1930 never made it out of committee to either the House or the Senate.

3. Blue-sky laws are state laws aimed at regulating the sale of securities. The categories of these laws were:
   A. fraud laws which imposed penalties for fraud in the sale of securities, and
   B. regulatory laws which prohibited the sale of securities until an application was filed and permission was granted by the state.

   These laws were ineffective because:
   A. Laws between states were not consistent.
   B. State legislatures were reluctant to enforce the laws.
   C. State laws contained numerous exemptions.

4. The practices of the 1920s which led to the erosion of the stock market were:
   A. price manipulation which gave false impressions of market activity and drove prices up, allowing profiteers large gains before prices fell back to their true market values.
   B. false and misleading statements which had as their objective the making of profits at the expense of unwary investors.
   C. extensive use of credit (large margins) which produced a slight market decline and started chain reactions which resulted in many investors not being able to cover their margins.
   D. misuse of information by corporate officials or "insiders" which involved the withholding of information until the officers could take advantage of it.

5. The primary function of the SEC is to ensure "full and fair" disclosure of all material facts concerning securities offered for public investment. Its purpose is not to prohibit speculative securities from entering the market,

but to insist investors be provided adequate information in order that they might make an informed decision.

6. Due to its legal authority to regulate the securities markets, the SEC has significant influence in securities markets activity. If anything, the SEC's role is likely to expand during the next decade.

7. The SEC is directed by five commissioners who are appointed by the President for a five-year term, one member's term expiring each year. Administered from the Washington, D.C., headquarters, the SEC has regional and branch offices in the major financial areas of the U.S. The major divisions of the SEC and their functions are:
   A. Division of Corporate Finance
      1. assists in establishing and regulating adherence to reporting and disclosure standards,
      2. sets standards for disclosure requirements of proxy solicitations, and
      3. provides interpretive and advisory service of requirements to professionals.
   B. Division of Market Regulation
      1. assists in regulation of national securities exchanges and brokers and dealers by
         a. attempting to discourage fraud or manipulation with the sale or purchase of securities and by
         b. supervising issuance of new securities,
      2. supervises broker-dealer inspection program, and
      3. provides interpretive advice to investors and registrants.
   C. Division of Enforcement
      1. supervises investigations and
      2. institutes injunctive actions.
   D. Division of Corporate Regulation
      1. helps administer the Public Utility Holding Company Act of 1935, and
      2. performs the Commission's advisory functions to the U.S. District Courts under Chapter X of the Bankruptcy Act.
   E. Division of Investment Management Regulation
      1. assists the SEC in administering the Investment Company Act of 1940 and the Investment Advisers Act of 1940, and
      2. supervises investigations arising from these acts.

8. Regional offices serve as field representatives for the Commission. They have the power to initiate investigations into possible violations and to conduct surprise investigations of brokers and dealers.

9. The Chief Accountant provides the Commission with expert advice in matters of accounting and auditing standards. The Chief Accountant has the statutory power to designate accounting principles and is the main liaison between the SEC and the accounting profession.

## CHAPTER 2

1. The primary acts governed by the SEC are the Securities Act of 1933 and the Securities Exchange Act of 1934. The secondary acts include: the Public Utility Holding Company Act of 1935, The Trust Indenture Act of 1939, the Investment Company Act of 1940, the Investment Advisers Act of 1940, the National Bankruptcy Act, Chapter X, and the Securities Investor Protection Act of 1970.

2. The basic objectives of the Securities Act of 1933 are:
   A. to provide investors with material financial and other information concerning securities offered for public sale, and
   B. to prohibit misrepresentation, deceit, and other fraudulent acts and practices in the sale of securities generally (whether or not required to be registered).

   These objectives are being met by:
   A. requiring any firm offering securities for sale to register with the SEC,
   B. imposing severe penalties for false or misleading information, and
   C. suing by investors through the courts for recovery of losses.

3. The major exemptions for registration under the 1933 Act and the categories in which these exemptions fall are the following:

|  | Exempted Securities | Exempted Transactions |
|---|---|---|
| A. Private offerings to a limited number of persons who do not propose to resell. | | X |
| B. Intrastate offerings. | | X |
| C. Offerings of municipal, governmental, or charitable businesses; banks, and common carriers. | X | |
| D. Offerings of limited size. | | X |
| E. Offerings of small business investment companies. | X | |

4. Though not a requirement of the 1933 Act or the SEC, a comfort letter is a document to the underwriter and to legal counsel stating that nothing has come to the attention of the auditor that would indicate the registration statements are false or misleading.

5. By passing the 1934 Act, Congress attempted to:
   A. regulate the trading of securities on secondary markets through brokers and exchanges and
   B. eliminate abuses in the trading of securities after their initial distribution.

   Congress also realized the necessity to have an organization to carry out the function of the law. With the Securities Exchange Act of 1934 the SEC was established.

6. The major differences in the requirements of the Securities Act of 1933 and the Securities Exchange Act of 1934 are:

| 1933 Act | 1934 Act |
|---|---|
| Registration of initial offerings | Continuation of reporting — firms and exchanges |
| Registration of issue | Registration of all exchanges, any security publicly traded, and brokers and dealers |
| Requirement of a prospectus | Prohibition of manipulative or deceptive devices |
| | Requirement of "insiders" to report holdings |

7. As measures to protect the investor, the SEC requires any investor who owns more than 10 percent of a registered company to:
   A. file report of holdings,
   B. report any changes in holdings, and
   C. recover to the company or shareholder any gains on short-term transactions.

8. A proxy is a written authorization allowing a person to act or to vote for another person, usually for a member of the board of directors. A proxy may not be solicited except under the rules the SEC may establish, and these rules require extensive disclosure.

9. The purposes of the regulations covering a tender offer are:
   A. to prevent surprise "take-over bids" and
   B. to allow time for the issuer to consider the tender offer.

10. The Federal Reserve Board can regulate margins by raising or lowering them, and investment can be stimulated or curtailed this way. Thus, the margin problems that contributed to the 1929 crash can now be controlled.

11. The disclosure tools used under the Public Utility Holding Company Act of 1935 are registration and reporting — the same as under the 1934 Act.

12. The major purposes of the Investment Company Act of 1940 and the Investment Advisers Act of 1940 are control and regulation of brokers and dealers and investment companies.

# CHAPTER 3

1. Basically, the registration process for the 1933 Act includes:
   A. selection of proper forms,
   B. request for a prefiling conference,
   C. submission of a registration statement,

    D. review by the SEC of the registration statement,

    E. preparation of the letter of comments,

    F. addition of amendments, if needed, and

    G. acceptance of an effective registration.

2. Since many statements are submitted for review, all members of the SEC's accounting staff are available to help advise registrants. Accountants should advise clients to take advantage of the available counsel; such action may help to save time and problems during the registration process.

3. The information required in the basic registration forms includes:

    A. the history and nature of the business,

    B. the capital structure of the business,

    C. the description of any material contracts,

    D. the description of securities being registered,

    E. the salaries and security holdings of major officers and directors,

    F. the underwriting arrangements,

    G. the estimate and use of net proceeds, and

    H. the financial statements.

4. The normal examination of a registration statement by the SEC consists of a review of the statement and a comparison with other information available. Such a review is done by the Division of Corporation Finance. A branch chief gives a copy of the statement to an accountant, a lawyer, and an analyst. Memoranda are submitted by each of these three experts, and a letter of comments is drafted.

5. The letter of comments outlines the deficiencies the review staff has found in the registration statement and makes comments as to how the document could be improved.

6. If a firm does not attempt to amend its original document, the SEC has three courses of action.

    A. It could let the statement become effective in deficient manner, and the company would be liable.

    B. It could issue a refusal order. Notice must be given within 10 days of filing and a hearing held in 10 days concerning corrections.

    C. It could issue a stop order. This halts further consideration of the statement.

7. The Division of Corporation Finance can select from four different review procedures.

    A. A deferred review is evoked when the statement is so deficient that review is closed unless the registrant proceeds.

    B. A cursory review is a simple review which reveals no deficiencies and no comments are made. The advisers of the registrant provide letters of acknowledgement.

    C. A summary review is a limited review, nearly the same as a cursory review.

    D. A customary review is the longer, more involved review.

8. While waiting for its registration statement to be accepted and declared effective, the company can make an announcement of the prospective issue of securities.

9. In a preliminary prospectus investment information must be disclosed, but information as to the offering price, commission to dealers, and other matters related to price is contained on a final prospectus. The name "red herring" is derived from the words "preliminary prospectus" stamped in red ink on the front page. This informs the investor that the SEC review is proceeding and that the issue is subject to it.

10. Although not a selling document, a "tombstone ad" is an advertisement such as those seen in the *Wall Street Journal* to locate the potential buyers.

11. To help prevent fraud by careful inquiry into the nature of the security being offered, the underwriters call a meeting of all involved professionals to discuss the issue. Final problems are resolved at this meeting.

12. The two major differences between the requirements under the 1933 Act and the 1934 Act involves the scope of registration and the extensive continuous reporting requirements under the 1934 Act.

# CHAPTER 4

1. Managements prepare two different annual reports, one for the SEC, the other for the investor.

2. The significant changes in disclosure include:
    A. The accounting profession and the SEC have recommended and encouraged increased disclosure.
    B. Audited financial statements are required to be sent to investors.
    C. Managements are cooperating better with the disclosure and reporting requirements.

3. Some of the recent disclosure requirements for annual reports are:
    A. audited financial statements for the last two fiscal years;
    B. summary of operations for the last five fiscal years and a management analysis thereof;
    C. a brief description of the business;
    D. a line-of-business or product line report for the last five fiscal years;
    E. identification of directors and executive officers with the principal occupation and employer of each;

F. identification of the principal market in which the securities of the firm are traded;

G. range of market prices and dividends for each quarter of the two most recent fiscal years; and

H. a free copy of the 10-K report to stockholders upon their written requests.

4. The most common forms sent to the SEC and the information contained on each are as follows:

| Form | Information Contained |
|---|---|
| S-1 | Information in prospectus<br>Other additional financial items |
| Proxy Statement | Information to be given in connection with proxy solicitation |
| 10-K | Annual financial reports |
| 10-Q | Quarterly financial reports |

5. The differences lie in the number of years for which a summary of operations is required and the number of years for which certified financial statements are required.

6. Form 8-K must be filed with the SEC within 10 days after the end of a month in which a significant material event has transpired.

7. Extent of detail, number of years for which information is required, and certification requirements are among the differences in reports sent to shareholders and those sent to the SEC.

# CHAPTER 5

1. The SEC has been granted broad statutory power
   A. to help it fulfill the goal of full and fair disclosure, and
   B. to help protect investors as a result of their dependence upon the opinion of experts such as accountants.

2. The SEC gradually attained the broad power it now possesses. When the abuses in securities markets caused the market crash of 1929, some people felt accounting principles were to blame. The first Congressional grant was given to the Federal Trade Commission in the Securities Act of 1933. The FTC was given the power to prescribe rules and procedures it deemed necessary to fulfill its obligations under the law. In 1934 the Securities Exchange Commission was established and received additional authority over companies filing reports. Under the Public Utility Holding Company Act of 1935, the SEC can not only specify the regulations but can even prescribe accounting systems to be used.

3. Regulation S-X is a codification of the views and requirements in relation to material to be filed with the SEC. Any accountant dealing with SEC work should have a current copy.

4. Accounting Series Releases primarily explain and clarify accounting procedures and practices needing special treatment in relation to disciplinary sanctions imposed by the SEC. Their purpose is to inform professionals of changing requirements and new SEC views.

5. Some of the instances where the SEC has exerted influence upon auditing standards and the significance of these influences are included below:

| Item | Significance |
|------|--------------|
| *McKesson-Robbins* Case | Resulted in standards for observing inventories and confirming receivables |
| *Yale Express* Case | Resulted in standards for disclosure of subsequent events previously certified |
| Concept of independence | Became part of the code of professional ethics |
| Fraud detection | Resulted in accountants being used more extensively as policing agents |
| Auditing procedures | Determined audit procedures |

6. The accounting profession's view is that the audit is not intended to detect fraud. Yet the SEC seems to be pushing auditors into the role of fraud detection.

7. The emphasis on legal liability can be attributed to several causes. First, managements and professionals have been subjected to damage suits stemming from their alleged negligence. Secondly, investors have been able to recoup their losses from the accountants or the managers who prepared and certified financial statements. And, more recently, an accountant's liability to third parties has been questioned. Then such precedent cases as *Ultramares Corporation, 1136 Tenants' Corporation, Continental Vending,* and *Barchris Construction Corporation* have focused more attention on legal liability.

8. Current emphasis on accountants' legal liability concerns
   A. liability to clients,
   B. liability to third parties,
   C. due professional care — ordinary vs. gross negligence —,
   D. awareness of current changes in auditing standards, and
   E. liability under the Securities Acts.

9. The essential objective of the SEC is to provide full and fair disclosure for investors. Therefore, the SEC has had a significant impact upon report-

ing requirements of businesses. The areas in which the SEC has evidenced influence include

A. segment reporting of diversified companies,

B. lease reporting, and

C. reporting of "significant business uncertainties."

10. The Commission's philosophy has been to let the accounting profession develop and promulgate its own principles and standards and to establish additional requirements when deemed necessary.

11. The current trend of the SEC action in regard to accounting principles seems to be the tendency to take over where there are gaps or inadequate standards. Refer to current events.

12. This is an opinion question. Certainly, there are good arguments for both sides. The author would argue for the private sector.